T0208926

THE POWERLESS CHURCH

America's National Disgrace

KATHE S. RUMSEY

WESTBOW
PRESS®
A DIVISION OF THOMAS NELSON
& ZONDERVAN

This book is a work of non-fiction. Unless otherwise noted, the author and the publisher make no explicit guarantees as to the accuracy of the information contained in this book and in some cases, names of people and places have been altered to protect their privacy.

WestBow Press books may be ordered through booksellers or by contacting:

WestBow Press
A Division of Thomas Nelson & Zondervan
1663 Liberty Drive
Bloomington, IN 47403
www.westbowpress.com
1 (866) 928-1240

Unless marked otherwise, all Scripture quotations are taken from the King James Version.

Scripture quotations marked NKJV are taken from the New King James Version®. Copyright © 1982 by Thomas Nelson. Used by permission. All rights reserved.

ISBN: 978-1-9736-9582-0 (sc)
ISBN: 978-1-9736-9581-3 (e)

Print information available on the last page.

WestBow Press rev. date: 7/1/2020

Thus were they defiled with their own works, and went a whoring with their own inventions. Therefore was the wrath of the LORD kindled against his people, insomuch that he abhorred his own inheritance. And he gave them into the hand of the heathen; and they that hated them ruled over them. Their enemies also oppressed them, and they were brought into subjection under their hand. Many times did he deliver them; but they provoked him with their counsel, and were brought low for their iniquity. Nevertheless he regarded their affliction, when he heard their cry: and he remembered for them his covenant, and repented according to the multitude of his mercies. He made them also to be pitied of all those that carried them captives. Save us, O LORD our God, and gather us from among the heathen, to give thanks unto thy holy name, and to triumph in thy praise. Blessed be the LORD God of Israel from everlasting to everlasting: and let all the people say, Amen. Praise ye the LORD.

—Psalm 106:39–48

Recognition

Truly, in everything, all glory belongs to God. Dedication of this book is to one of God's faithful sons, Allen StandingBear Jenkins. Professor Jenkins exemplifies God's heart as mentor and teacher. His integrity inspired his students in the most uncompromising manner to seek truth.

Contents

Introduction

Most people who listen to the news media have become acutely aware of the ominous challenges within our nation. If it were not for faith in God, and a personal relationship with our Lord Jesus Christ, I believe many would easily lose all hope.

Following the 2008 presidential election, I falsely assumed America was going through her customary election year cycle of disturbances. However, years later, I reflect upon the bleak condition of our nation. In light of our drifting from America's founding principles, I struggle to make sense of our options. Unresolved challenges evolve into one impasse after another. Bogus attempts by elected officials to work together have become a thing of the past. Showmanship banter fails to shore up our nation's foundation.

Only God knows what season of history we now face. Only He can provide the wisdom needed to restore our homeland's former splendor. The church and America face a pivotal moment of decision. Our nation's future lies in the hands of those of us who call ourselves Christians. Like generations before us, I believe when the faithful church humbled herself before God and prayed, His merciful hand moved and He delayed His judgment. "If my people, which are called by my name, shall humble themselves, and pray, and seek my face, and turn from their wicked ways; then will I hear from heaven, and will forgive their sin, and will heal their land" *(2 Chronicles 7:14)*.

If the church continues to conform to the world's idols and commits spiritual adultery, God's intervention to bless this nation remains delusional thinking. As our nation crumbles under our feet, weekly church services filled with society's wisdom do nothing more than appease our soulish nature. The power of the gospel of Jesus Christ and the kingdom of God remain a mystery to most church members. The hour is late; we no longer have the luxury of time to waste on fruitless pursuits.

Word spoken to my spirit in 1988 by the Holy Spirit:

The battle has begun. Put on the armor of God daily. Love the Lord God with all of your heart. There can be no other gods before Me. My children must love one another more than they ever thought possible—enough, I say, that they be willing to lay down their life, one for another—You see so much, yet see so little. Trust, walk cheerfully My way. It won't be much longer. You must decide to go on knowing all is well.

Trust, trust, trust. My beautiful trust is the key. A loving father establishes a trust for his children so that their needs will be met even in his absence. Would I do less? Trust Me. I love you greatly. If only My children could comprehend My love as Jesus did, Satan would not have such a hold on their lives. They would take the authority I have given them. Take it now and use it widely. There is much to do, but you need not hurry. I do all things in My time. I can speed it up, I can slow it down. Go at My pace. Do not struggle. Do not worry. All is well.

Cleanse
(Matthew 23:25–28; Luke 11:39)

Hopes and Dreams

Our founding fathers shared a dream for America in her infancy. Solid faith in God influenced their decision to establish a life in the new land upon their biblical convictions. The pursuit of life, liberty and happiness compelled men and women to sacrifice for these noble goals. Freedom from tyranny became more valuable than comfort.

Evidenced over the past fifty years, compromise has lulled our nation and the church to sleep, camouflaging ungodly influences. Satan's kingdom has taken a foothold *(Ephesians 6:12)*. While the passive church accommodated the world, she became entangled and powerless. God's name and presence vanished from almost every aspect of our nation. No longer welcomed in American public life, His righteousness disappeared from the actions of mankind. Biblical principles departed as churches compromised God's Word, and prayerlessness took root. The church's authority sits idle. Furthermore, to retain her tax-exempt advantages, the church exchanged her Rock-solid foundation for sinking sand.

It has become increasingly easy to blame our government and its politicians for America's demise. However, contrary to popular opinion, politics is not the force for change that Americans need. A revival within the heart of every believer is the answer. The plank in our eye causes us to misjudge everything around us. If we truly want God to restore America to her former glory, Christians must repent and pray. We must examine ourselves honestly in spirit, mind, and body *(Titus 2:11–15; 3:1–11; Jude vs. 3–5, 11–13)*. Are we light and salt? Conversely, has our salt lost its flavor? Our nation's restoration solely depends upon believers acting responsibly and faithfully to the Word of God. Change begins and must come from within each member of the body of Christ.

> Behold, ye trust in lying words, that cannot profit. Will ye steal, murder, and commit adultery, and swear falsely, and burn incense unto Ba'al, and walk after other gods whom ye know not; and come and stand before me in this house, which is called by my name, and say, We are delivered to do all these abominations? Is this house, which is called by my name, become a den of robbers in your eyes? Behold, even I have seen it, saith the LORD.
>
> —*Jeremiah 7:8–11*

Foreign Settlers

To understand how far the nation has fallen from our founders' ideals, we must understand their motivations that brought them here. They were not seeking free handouts or government intervention. They sought a new land free from religious oppression. These foreign settlers understood the risks and voluntarily sacrificed their lives and worldly possessions to worship God freely. With singleness of purpose, their desire to love God openly compelled them to forsake all. These settlers willingly paid the price.

In Jeremiah chapter two, we read that the entire nation of Israel had forsaken God. To awaken their senses, God asked the people what iniquity He committed to receive such rejection. He mercifully reminds them how He rescued them from oppression through "a land that no man passed through, and where no man dwelt" into a bountiful country.

This, too, is true of America's beginnings. European foreigners sailed through a wilderness of unknown waters to arrive on the shores of a plentiful land, blessed of God. Sadly, however, like Israel, our arrogance pushed God from every public arena after experiencing His many blessings.

In God Is Our Trust

God is love, and He loves unconditionally. He provides multiple opportunities to reconsider and repent from our poor choices. If we draw close to God, He will draw near to us *(James 4:8)*. God promises in *2 Chronicles 7:14* if we humble ourselves and pray, and seek Him, and turn from sin, then He will heal our land. This is a powerful verse. He alone possesses the ability to turn harmful circumstances around for good *(Romans 8:28)*. Yet without the church's cooperation, there remains little hope for our ailing nation and her future generations.

Some Christians believe we have already missed our opportunity. However, since God looks at our heart, He willingly accepts the prayers of a remnant *(Proverbs 4:23; Mark 11:23)*. Through repentance and the intercession of the church, America's future does not have to remain in a downward spiral *(Jeremiah 29:11; James 5:17–18)*. Prayers of faith bring bright prospects. We must choose to serve God in light, and not Satan in darkness.

Through his divisive tactics, the Devil knows he can obstruct God's evangelistic plans for our nation, while he demoralizes America's foundation. Satan knows that any kingdom, house, or country divided against itself will not stand. False accusations and slander that focus on differences not only polarize ethnicities, but also breed division *(Matthew 12:25; Ephesians 6:12)*. The ideals of freedom of speech exclude slander. The problems within our nation originate not from a man's ethnic background, but from his heart. We are all of one human race.

Scripture states that God "hath made of one blood all nations of men for to dwell on all the face of the earth, and hath determined the times before appointed, and the bounds of their habitation; that they should seek the LORD, if haply they might feel after him, and find him, though he be not far from every one of us" *(Acts 17:26–27)*.

Compromise Destroys Our Strength
Idolatry within the church makes us indistinguishable from the world. Jesus warned of hypocrisy and said, "Ye are they which justify yourselves before men; but God knoweth your hearts: for that which is highly esteemed among men is abomination in the sight of God" *(Luke 16:15)*. Individually, we must examine the motives of our heart. Are we truly serving God or mammon? The enemy can too easily deceive us *(James 4:4)*.

> But there were false prophets also among the people, even as there shall be false teachers among you, who privily shall bring in damnable heresies, even denying the Lord that bought them, and bring upon themselves swift destruction. And many shall follow their pernicious ways; by reason of whom the way of truth shall be evil spoken of.
> *—2 Peter 2:1–2*

> For when they speak great swelling words of vanity, they allure through the lusts of the flesh, through much wantonness, those that were clean escaped from them who live in error.
> *—2 Peter 2:18*

Kathe S. Rumsey

When we attempt to remedy our nation's present-day problems with situational ethics, thereby sugarcoating sin, spirits of antichrist operate unrestrained *(1 John 2:18–21)*. For this to occur in a nation whose leaders once honored God without reservation demonstrates the church's prayerlessness and disregard for truth.

For if God spared not the angels that sinned, but cast them down to hell, and delivered them into chains of darkness, to be reserved unto judgment; and spared not the old world, but saved Noah the eighth person, a preacher of righteousness, bringing in the flood upon the world of the ungodly; and turning the cities of Sodom and Go-mor'rha into ashes condemned them with an overthrow, making them an ensample [example] unto those that after should live ungodly; and delivered just Lot, vexed with the filthy conversation of the wicked: (For that righteous man dwelling among them, in seeing and hearing, vexed his righteous soul from day to day with their unlawful deeds); The Lord knoweth how to deliver the godly out of temptations, and to reserve the unjust unto the day of judgment to be punished: But chiefly them that walk after the flesh in the lust of uncleanness, and despise government [authority]. Presumptuous are they, selfwilled, they are not afraid to speak evil of dignities.

—2 Peter 2:4–10

God has called His church with a holy calling, set apart to love and serve Him. We are to worship Him alone *(Luke 4:8)*. To condone or conform to popular opinion or trends will not solve the problems of our nation or the church *(2 John vs. 7–11)*.

If we truly trust God the Father, then we must honor Him. We need His wisdom and the Word of God to direct us for all that is ahead. We must hear from heaven. Obedience to God alone will restore the church and our land *(2 Timothy 3:1–9; Philippians 4:19; Luke 12:22–31)*. Jesus is the way, the truth, and the life *(John 14:6)*. "Neither is there salvation in any other" *(Acts 4:12)*.

> A voice was heard upon the high places, weeping and supplications of the children of Israel: for they have perverted their way, and they have forgotten the LORD their God.
>
> —*Jeremiah 3:21*

> Turn, O backsliding children, saith the LORD; for I am married [to rule over] unto you: and I will take you one of a city, and two of a family, and I will bring you to Zion: and I will give you pastors according to mine heart, which shall feed you with knowledge and understanding.
>
> —*Jeremiah 3:14–15*

Jeremiah, known as the weeping prophet, struggled emotionally within his prophetic office. A rebellious nation that walked in debauchery rejected his message to repent of their evil ways. Considering her current state of affairs—like Israel—God has a timely message of repentance to the United States of America—a wakeup call. Individually, believers must repent and cleanse God's temple from within, that is, our own hearts *(1 Corinthians 6:19)*.

In the last day, that great day of the feast, Jesus stood and cried, saying, If any man thirst, let him come unto me, and drink. He that believeth on me, as the scripture hath said, out of his belly shall flow rivers of living water.

—*John 7:37–38*

But ye shall receive power, after that the Holy Ghost is come upon you: and ye shall be witnesses unto me both in Jerusalem, and in all Judæa, and in Sa-mâ'ri-a, and unto the uttermost part of the earth.

—*Acts 1:8*

And the multitude of them that believed were of one heart and of one soul: neither said any of them that ought of the things which he possessed was his own; but they had all things common. And with great power gave the apostles witness of the resurrection of the Lord Jesus: and great grace was upon them all.

—*Acts 4:32–33*

Spirit

Watch and pray, that ye enter not into temptation: the
spirit indeed is willing, but the flesh is weak.

—Matthew 26:41

Power over Weakness

Each day offers a new beginning to serve either God or the world; we
make our own choices. How many times have we found ourselves
watching a news program only to have biased reporting agitate us?
Evil reports, let alone falsehoods, should compel us to turn off our
televisions and computers and seek truth in God's Word. We have
opportunities to redeem our time in prayer and Bible study.

In this hour of uncertainty and turmoil, believers need the
encouragement of one another. Just as iron sharpens iron, we must
edify one another in the Lord *(Proverbs 27:17; Matthew 18:19–
20; Hebrews 10:23–25).* God's people are the body of Christ here
on earth. We are His house of prayer, and Jesus has passed His
scepter of authority to us. The authority He gave the church must
not sit idle *(Matthew 28:18; John 14:12).*

Whatever believers bind on earth is bound in heaven. Whatever
we allow to take place on the earth Is allowed in the kingdom of
heaven *(Matthew 16:19).* Because Jesus has overcome the world,
His expectation is that we will do the same *(John 16:33).* We
must live by faith in Christ and finish our race. As joint heirs with
Him, we reign in this life overcoming the world *(Romans 5:17).*
Jesus Christ is King over all the earth *(Psalm 47:2; John 18:37;
Revelation 19:16).*

And he [Jesus] cometh, and findeth them sleeping,
and saith unto Peter, Simon, sleepest thou? couldest

not thou watch one hour? Watch ye and pray, lest ye
enter into temptation. The spirit truly is ready, but the
flesh is weak.

—*Mark 14:37–38*

As I read *Mark 14:37*, the word *hour* leaped out. I have learned
that when a word in Scripture grabs my attention, the Holy Spirit
is at work. My response is to dig deeper to understand what He is
teaching me. "But the Comforter, which is the Holy Ghost, whom
the Father will send in my name, he shall teach you all things, and
bring all things to your remembrance, whatsoever I have saith
unto you" *(John 14:26)*.

God has a plan for our lives. We have only one lifetime to
fulfill His purpose. *Ecclesiastes 3:1* tells us, "To every thing
there is a season, and a time to every purpose under heaven."
"Who [God] hath saved us, and called us with an holy calling,
not according to our works, but according to his own purpose
and grace, which was given us in Christ Jesus before the world
began" *(2 Timothy 1:9)*. To fulfill God's will, we must redeem
our time wisely. It is our responsibility to train our ears to hear
the Holy Spirit.

Little children, it is the last time: and as ye have heard
that antichrist shall come, even now are there many
antichrists; whereby we know that it is the last time.

—*1 John 2:18*

A New Creation

The church cannot expect others to understand our perspective
of life. Unless a person is born again of God, regenerated in one's
spirit, it is impossible for them to understand our biblical point of

view. We only understand the spiritual principles of the kingdom of God when the Holy Spirit of truth reveals them to us *(John 16:13–14).*

> Jesus answered and said unto him [Nicodemus], Verily, verily, I say unto thee, Except a man be born again, he cannot see the kingdom of God. That which is born of the flesh is flesh; and that which is born of the Spirit is spirit.
>
> *—John 3:3, 6*

Jesus sent His disciples to preach the good news, the gospel of God. His goal was to teach truths of the kingdom of God, mysteries previously hidden *(Ephesians 3:1–12).* After His departure from earth, Jesus asked God the Father to send the Spirit of truth, the Holy Spirit, to be our helper and teacher. He is the one who reveals God's will for our life. Today is the day of salvation. Now is the time to,

- be born again, born of the Spirit *(John 3:3–8)*
- be filled with the Holy Spirit *(Matthew 3:11; Acts 2:4)*
- hear, and obey God's plan for us personally *(Matthew 6:10; Revelation 2:7)*

> Marvel not that I said unto thee, Ye must be born again. The wind bloweth where it listeth, and thou hearest the sound thereof, but canst not tell whence it cometh, and whither it goeth: so is every one that is born of the Spirit.
>
> *—John 3:7–8*

Kathe S. Rumsey

Individually, believers must ask, "Am I truly born again or have I inherited my salvation through my family who have always attended church services?"

I grew up in a Christian home and a traditional denomination, but it was not until I was in my early thirties that I experienced a personal encounter with God that resulted in a life-changing awareness of Him. It was an undeniable reality of God's conviction of my sin of pride and self-centeredness, while at the same time a manifestation of His unconditional love for me. His outpouring of the Spirit of grace upon me changed me and my life forever.

> And the Word was made flesh, and dwelt among us, (and we beheld his glory, the glory of the only begotten of the Father,) full of grace and truth.
>
> —*John 1:14*

> For he [Jesus] whom God hath sent speaketh the words of God: for God giveth not the Spirit by measure unto him. The Father loveth the Son, and hath given all things into his hand. He that believeth on the Son hath everlasting life: and he that believeth not the Son shall not see life; but the wrath of God abideth on him.
>
> —*John 3:34–36*

As I read the word *measure* in this verse, the Holy Spirit quickened it to my spirit. I realized we could limit the Holy Spirit by our choices. Measure also appears in *Romans 12:3*, "God hath dealt to every man the measure of faith." We can build our faith through prayer and the Word of God *(Jude vs. 20)*.

The Holy Spirit is a gentleman. Our Father in heaven sent Him to comfort and teach us. However, I sometimes hear discourses among church members regarding programs to "bring others to Christ," or to "build the kingdom of God." Yet since the 1990s, I have experienced only a handful of occasions in which the Holy Spirit freely operated among the Christian congregations I visited. His presence is sometimes apparent during praise and worship time, but afterwards the Holy Spirit seems quite still. I ask myself why this is so prevalent if God does not give the Holy Spirit by measure.

Holy Spirit's Role in the Church

If God is not restricting the availability of His Spirit, then the responsibility rests upon our shoulders. If we do not resist the will of the Holy Spirit, but allow Him to move freely, God the Father will draw people to Jesus *(John 6:44)*. Church members must reject man-made programs that mirror the world's idols just to increase church attendance. These only compromise the power of the gospel.

Man's ways are not God's ways. Christ alone is head of His church. Individually and corporately, the church must submit to Him in everything if we desire fruitful lives.

The conviction of the Holy Spirit of God upon the human heart is the only action that can bring an individual to true repentance and salvation. If we hope to see others saved and baptized with the Holy Spirit, then we the church must search our own hearts, repent, and turn from our evil ways. If true honor of God and His Word is the foundation that made America great, then the church needs to examine her current role.

Let no man deceive you with vain words: for because of these things cometh the wrath of God upon the children of disobedience. Be not ye therefore partakers with them. For ye were sometimes darkness, but now are ye light in the Lord: walk as children of light: (For the fruit of the Spirit is in all goodness and righteousness and truth;) proving what is acceptable unto the Lord. And have no fellowship with the unfruitful works of darkness, but rather reprove [expose] them. For it is a shame even to speak of those things which are done of them in secret. But all things that are reproved are made manifest by the light: for whatsoever doth make manifest is light. Wherefore he saith, Awake thou that sleepest, and arise from the dead, and Christ shall give thee light. See then that ye walk circumspectly, not as fools, but as wise, redeeming the time, because the days are evil. Wherefore be ye not unwise, but understanding what the will of the Lord is. And be not drunk with wine, wherein is excess; but be filled with the Spirit.

—Ephesians 5:6–18

Deceived by Intellectual Charade

Scripture soundly warns the church in *2 Peter 2:1–3* to beware of false teachers. The world, as well as the church, falsely assumes these charlatans possess special wisdom and knowledge. Intellectually and emotionally seduced by persuasive speeches, the world and the church fall prey to falsehoods. Without the Spirit of truth and the wisdom of God, all of us can be deceived. Wise choices require critical thinking skills and the light of God's Word. Christians must not buy into the slick marketed programs offered by hirelings who are disguised in sheep's clothing within the church *(John 10:12; 1 Corinthians 2:1–13)*.

Likewise, the popularity and appealing appearances of actors and athletes seduce many in our culture. They are extravagantly well paid, yet we know actors are not the same people they portray in the movies, nor do athletes possess extraordinary abilities many imagine. None of these individuals perform supernatural exploits nor defeat entire armies single handedly. Some haughtily or even humorously claim to be atheists.

Yet the One who made himself of no reputation, Jesus Christ, the Son of God, is King of kings; presently, Jesus sits at the right hand of the throne of God *(Colossians 3:1)*. In Him "are hid all the treasures of wisdom and knowledge" *(John 1:14; Colossians 2:3)*. Christ is "the power and the wisdom of God" *(1 Corinthians 1:24)*.

Jesus never told people what they wanted to hear; He told them what they needed to hear. Yet we know He had compassion toward all. God's wisdom comes from above and "is first pure, then peaceable, gentle, and easy to be intreated, full of mercy and good fruits, without partiality and without hypocrisy" *(James 3:17)*.

Ephesians 5:6 warns us not to be deceived with vain words. Flattery appeals to our emotions, but the truth spoken in love edifies the church. Flattery, which is deceptive and manipulative, proceeds from an evil heart. Christians must understand what the Lord's will is for us in this evil day. The Holy Spirit will instruct us with the Word of God.

> All scripture is given by inspiration of God, and is profitable for doctrine, for reproof, for correction, for instruction in righteousness: that the man of God may be perfect, throughly furnished unto all good work.
> —*2 Timothy 3:16*

Kathe S. Rumsey

Guidance for Successful Living

The Bible, God's reference manual—corrects—instructs—and provides direction for the church. If God's children fail to read the training manual He provided, it is impossible to expect our lives to improve. How many times have we brought a product home to assemble—ripped open the box—pulled out all the parts in random order and started to assemble the pieces before looking at the instruction manual? I lived thirty-four years before I found the instructions for my life, and yet they lay hidden in the Bible the entire time.

> God is a Spirit: and they that worship him must worship him in spirit and in truth.
>
> —*John 4:24*

Jesus Christ is the Word of God. The Word "was made flesh and dwelt among us" *(John 1:1, 14)*. Jesus taught, "The words [rhema] that I speak unto you, they are spirit, and they are life" *(John 6:63)*. Because God's Word is truth, and we receive revelation of it by hearing the Holy Spirit, then our obedience to what we hear is true worship.

As Christians who profess to know Jesus as Lord, do we remain faithful to His words when life becomes complicated? Jesus emphasized the pathway that leads to life would be difficult *(Matthew 7:14; 16:24)*. Since persecutions and troubles come for the Word's sake, it is through these challenging times, we must walk by faith, not by sight.

> But if we hope for that we see not, then do we with patience wait for it. Likewise the Spirit also helpeth our

infirmities: for we know not what we should pray for as we ought: but the Spirit itself maketh intercession for us with groanings which cannot be uttered. And he that searcheth the hearts knoweth what is the mind of the Spirit, because he maketh intercession for the saints according to the will of God. And we know that all things work together for good to them that love God, to them who are the called according to his purpose.

—*Romans 8:25–28*

Wait for the Father's Promise

After Jesus' resurrection from the dead, He commanded His disciples to wait for God the Father's promise, "for John truly baptized with water, but ye shall be baptized with the Holy Ghost" *(Acts 1:5).*

And they were all filled with the Holy Ghost, and began to speak with other tongues, as the Spirit gave them utterance.

—*Acts 2:4*

The promise of God the Father—the Holy Spirit—will dramatically change anyone's prayer life. God is no respecter of persons. If believers desire to have this gift, our heavenly Father will give the Holy Spirit to those who ask *(Mark 16:17; Luke 11:13; Acts 10:44–46; 19:6; 1 Corinthians 12:10–11, 27–28).* Just as Jesus depended upon and obeyed the Holy Spirit during His life on earth, Christians must have ears to hear what the Spirit is saying to the present-day church.

Kathe S. Rumsey

For as many as are led by the Spirit of God, they are sons [mature] of God. For ye have not received the spirit of bondage again to fear; but ye have received the Spirit of adoption, whereby we cry, Abba, Father.

—Romans 8:14–15

Feed My Sheep

America's churches of all denominations consistently raise finances to send and support their missionaries around the world. Yet, many fail to feed the flock at home, robbing congregations of their spiritual sustenance. Many churches neglect to practice the fundamental principles of Christ's doctrine *(Hebrews 6:1–2)*. Sadly, many of the redeemed believers do not know who they are in Christ.

When was the last time we heard a pastor offer prayer for members to receive Jesus Christ as their personal Lord and Savior, let alone to receive the baptism with the Holy Spirit? *(Romans 10:9–10)*. As Christians, we are vessels of God's anointing. Are we on fire for God, or aimlessly walking on a religious treadmill? Is the Word of God alive in our hearts? Are we students of His Word? *(2 Timothy 2:15)*.

Paul said to the people of Corinth, "I, brethren, could not speak unto you as unto spiritual, but as carnal, even as unto babes in Christ. I have fed you with milk, and not with meat; for hitherto ye were not able to bear it, neither yet now are ye able. For ye are yet carnal: for whereas there is among you envying, strife, and divisions, are ye not carnal, and walk as men? *(1 Corinthians 3:1–3; Hebrews 5:12–14)*.

Then Peter said unto them, Repent, and be baptized every one of you in the name of Jesus Christ for the remission of sins, and ye shall receive the gift of the Holy Ghost. For the promise is unto you, and to your children, and to all that are afar off, even as many as the Lord our God shall call.

—Acts 2:38–39

The Word of God Contains All Solutions

God's abundant wisdom is available to His church to correct the enormous problems that erode America's foundation. Through the prayers of Jesus' church, God has granted His people the keys of authority both in heaven and on earth. Jesus admonishes us to pray; He calls His church "the house of prayer" *(Matthew 21:13)*. The critical means necessary—the Word of God and the Holy Spirit—equip us to pray victoriously. God highly exalted His Son, giving Jesus a name above all names *(Philippians 2:9)*. Knowing this, faith says, "With God all things are possible" *(Matthew 19:26)*. Therefore, restoration of America begins with the revival of each believer's heart.

The church can impact our communities and nation for good when we humble ourselves and honor God. When believers obey His inspired Word, the Lord will intervene and heal our land. His ears are open to the prayers of the righteous. We must not limit God by our stubborn refusal to study His Word and pray. Only God can resolve our nation's problems and restore her. Patiently, the Holy Spirit waits for the body of Christ to seek God's wisdom in prayer and then obey it.

And it shall come to pass in the last days, saith God, I will pour out of my Spirit upon all flesh: and your sons and your daughters shall prophesy, and your young men shall see visions, and your old men shall dream dreams: and on my servants and on my handmaidens I will pour out in those days of my Spirit; and they shall prophesy; And it shall come to pass, that whosoever shall call on the name of the Lord shall be saved.

—Acts 2:17–18, 21

Mind

One person esteems one day above another; another
esteems every day alike. Let each be fully convinced
in his own mind. He who observes the day, observes
it to the Lord; and he who does not observe the day,
to the Lord he does not observe it. He who eats, eats
to the Lord, for he gives God thanks; and he who
does not eat, to the Lord he does not eat, and gives
God thanks. For none of us lives to himself, and no
one dies to himself. For if we live, we live to the
Lord; and if we die, we die to the Lord. Therefore,
whether we live or die, we are the Lord's. For to
this end Christ died and rose and lived again, that
He might be Lord of both the dead and the living.
But why do you judge your brother? Or why do you
show contempt for your brother? For we shall all
stand before the judgment seat of Christ. For it is
written: As I live, says the LORD, Every knee shall
bow to Me, and every tongue shall confess to God.
So then each of us shall give account of himself
to God.

—Romans 14:5–12 (NKJV)

As believers, we should not be mentally or physically preoccupied
with the cares of this life. At any moment, our time on earth
may end. In a twinkling of an eye, we could find ourselves face
to face with our Lord and Savior Jesus Christ. If we knew we
were to take our last breath on earth, how would we spend our
remaining hours? Often when I find myself overwhelmed by the
needs around me, this thought paces back and forth through my

mind. When I look at my time on this earth as being finite, it helps me prioritize and simplify my life.

> I BESEECH you therefore, brethren, by the mercies of God, that ye present your bodies a living sacrifice, holy, acceptable unto God, which is your reasonable service. And be not conformed to this world: but be ye transformed by the renewing of your mind, that ye may prove what is that good, and acceptable, and perfect, will of God.
>
> —*Romans 12:1–2*

Only God knows how much I must rely upon Him to accomplish what He wants me to complete. In the flesh—ideas and projects flow liberally through my mind—presenting me with many opportunities. Nevertheless, what I consider God's will for my life—based upon His order of relationships—influences what I accomplish. His kingdom protocol reminds me why God blessed me with my precious husband, and my dear friend and prayer partner. I know He placed these two individuals in my life to provide a way of escape from worldly distractions and procrastination.

Division Among Us

> Now I beseech you, brethren, by the name of our Lord Jesus Christ, that ye all speak the same thing, and that there be no divisions among you; but that ye be perfectly joined together in the same mind and in the same judgment. For it hath been declared unto me of you, my brethren, by them which are of the house of Chlo'e, that there are contentions among you.

Now this I say, that every one of you saith, I am of Paul; and I of Apollos; and I of Ce'phas; and I of Christ. Is Christ divided? was Paul crucified for you? or were ye baptized in the name of Paul? I thank God that I baptized none of you, but Crispus and Gaius; lest any should say that I had baptized in mine own name. For Christ sent me not to baptize, but to preach the gospel: not with wisdom of words, lest the cross of Christ should be made of none effect. For the preaching of the cross is to them that perish foolishness; but unto us which are saved it is the power of God. For it is written, I will destroy the wisdom of the wise, and will bring to nothing the understanding of the prudent. Where is the wise? where is the scribe? where is the disputer of this world? hath not God made foolish the wisdom of this world? For after that in the wisdom of God the world by wisdom knew not God, it pleased God by the foolishness of preaching to save them that believe.

—1 Corinthians 1:10–15, 17–21

Before we, the church, blame America's downfall on strife and divisions within our nation's institutions, we must examine ourselves. In *John 17:21*, Jesus' prayer demonstrates His desire for unity within His church. He and the Father are one. Sadly, some may continue to say, I am Baptist; I am Catholic; I am Assembly of God; I am Lutheran, or some other denomination. To some, one's identity with a specific denomination translates into salvation and eternal life. This kind of thinking only breeds division and elitism within the body of Christ. Jesus Christ alone is the author of eternal salvation *(Hebrews 5:9).*

Does denominationalism fit God's plan for His church? When I questioned the concept of denominations, a pastor once responded, "God is all about order." I knew I could not refute his statement. God has an established order. However, to focus upon a denomination as to identify with it without regard to its doctrine jeopardizes one's salvation. To allow it to define one's faith only highlights the divisions within the body of Christ *(Ephesians 2:8)*.

In the Book of Revelation, Jesus delivered a specific message to each of the seven churches located in various cities. It would be like saying, *To the church in Houston*, or *To the church in New York*, or *To the church in Paris*. God never distinguishes His church—His people—by denomination. This should make one examine and question the source and causes of denominational divisions *(2 Timothy 2:15)*. Are they doctrinally sound? *(John 7:16–18; Hebrews 6:1–2)*. It is no wonder many Christians—as well as the unsaved—are confused about the gospel of Jesus Christ.

Thirty-seven years ago, I attended a church conference sponsored by a different Christian denomination than the one in which I attended at the time. However, it was at this service that I was born-again and baptized with the Holy Spirit. For me to have denied God's presence and reject Him and the work of His Holy Spirit because of my unfamiliar surroundings would have been foolish. Holding onto unsound denominational doctrine limits God.

> This people draweth nigh unto me with their mouth, and honoureth me with their lips, but their heart is far from me. But in vain they do worship me, teaching for doctrines the commandments of men.
>
> —*Matthew 15:8–9*

If Jesus Christ returned to earth within the next twenty-four hours, what denominational church do you think He would visit? Would He first go to Springfield, Utah, or Rome? Would He wash the pope's feet or vice versa? Would Jesus schedule His return to earth so He could attend the annual Southern Baptist Convention? These questions sound silly, but they are to challenge us to think, to search the Scriptures for ourselves (*1 John 2:27–29*). If we want to understand God's will for our lives, and know who we are in Christ, what denomination should we join, if any? Scripture teaches two believers in prayer set God's will into motion. Where two or three come together in His name, Jesus will be with us *(Matthew 18:19–20)*.

> And he taught, saying unto them, Is it not written, My house shall be called of all nations the house of prayer? but ye have made it a den of thieves.
>
> *—Mark 11:17*

> Ep'a-phras, who is one of you, a servant of Christ, saluteth you, always labouring fervently for you in prayers, that ye may stand perfect and complete in all the will of God. For I bear him record, that he hath a great zeal for you, and them that are in La-od-i-ce'a, and them in Hi-e-rap'o-lis. Luke, the beloved physician, and Demas, greet you. Salute the brethren which are in La-od-i-ce'a, and Nym'-phas, and the church that is in his house. And when this epistle is read among you, cause that it be read also in the church of the La-od-i-ce'ans; and that ye likewise read the epistle from La-od-i-ce'a. And say to Ar-chip'pus, Take heed to the ministry which thou hast received in the Lord, that

thou fulfil it. The salutation by the hand of me Paul. Remember my bonds. Grace be with you. Amen.

—Colossians 4:12–18

Lukewarm Church

Jesus described the church in Laodicea as being neither hot nor cold. Members of this church viewed themselves as rich, prosperous, in need of nothing. Yet the Lord referred to them as "wretched, and miserable, and poor, and blind, and naked" *(Revelation 3:17)*.

Outward appearances must not deceive the body of Christ. Some churches may appear strong and prosperous, but remember Jesus cursed the fig tree because it produced no fruit *(Matthew 21:19–22)*.

We must pray that God never lets us forget the time when we were first born-again. For me, it was a time of being so on fire for God that nothing could stop me from sharing His truth with everyone I knew. We need only to experience the redeeming grace of Jesus Christ to tell others what is so real in our own heart *(Roman 10:10)*. After experiencing the presence of God through His Holy Spirit, nothing could deter my pursuit of a personal relationship with Him.

> And be not conformed to this world: but be ye transformed by the renewing of your mind, that ye may prove what is that good, and acceptable, and perfect will of God.
>
> *—Romans 12:2*

Idols Within the Church

> Be ye not unequally yoked together with unbelievers: for what fellowship hath righteousness with

unrighteousness? and what communion hath light with darkness? and what concord hath Christ with Be'li-al? or what part hath he that believeth with an infidel? and what agreement hath the temple of God with idols? for ye are the temple of the living God; as God hath said, I will dwell in them, and walk in them; and I will be their God, and they shall be my people. Wherefore come out from among them, and be ye separate, saith the Lord, and touch not the unclean thing; and I will receive you, and will be a Father unto you, and ye shall be my sons and daughters, saith the Lord Almighty.

—2 Corinthians 6:14–18

If believers are the temple of God, what part do we have with idols? Present-day merchandise advertisements are highly refined and alluring to the unsuspecting Christian. With over forty years of marketing and business experience, it breaks my heart to see people base their self-worth upon the accumulation of specific brands and the latest product trends. What disturbs me even more is the association these products have with the gods of this world.

As a former merchandise buyer for a specialty department store, I learned early in my career to follow emerging trends through the merchandise trade markets and professional publications. It was our responsibility as purchasing agents to stay at least a year ahead of the consuming public. Our focus was to meet their needs and provide our customers with the newest product knowledge. Times have changed, and the focus now is on marketing an emotional response. Consumers, blindly led through one marketing experience after another, become thoroughly convinced that what they presently own is outdated. To focus on the things of this world and to give them priority in our lives is idolatry.

Be Mindful of God's Priorities

Let love be without dissimulation. Abhor that which is evil; cleave to that which is good. Be kindly affectioned one to another with brotherly love; in honour preferring one another; not slothful in business; fervent in spirit; serving the Lord; rejoicing in hope; patient in tribulation; continuing instant in prayer; distributing to the necessity of saints; given to hospitality. Bless them which persecute you: bless, and curse not. Rejoice with them that do rejoice, and weep with them that weep. Be of the same mind one toward another. Mind not high things, but condescend to men of low estate. Be not wise in your own conceits.

—Romans 12:9–16

Body

But he that is joined unto the Lord is one spirit. Flee fornication. Every sin that a man doeth is without the body; but he that committeth fornication sinneth against his own body. What? know ye not that your body is the temple of the Holy Ghost which is in you, which ye have of God, and ye are not your own? For ye are bought with a price: therefore glorify God in your body, and in your spirit, which are God's.

—*1 Corinthians 6:17–20*

The 1970s Ushered in Change

Bombarded with the slogan "Your right to choose," and then indoctrinated with, "Your body is yours to do with as you please," America—as we had known her—changed.

God's Word tells us Jesus Christ redeemed us through His death on the cross. We are not our own. No matter how hard the world tries to convince us, they will never change God's mind. We must resist the uncertainty of our emotions and worldly wisdom. God abhors all manner of evil.

But thou hast played the harlot with many lovers; yet return again to me, saith the Lord. Therefore the showers have been withholden, and there hath been no latter rain; and thou hadst a whore's forehead, thou refusedst to be ashamed.

—*Jeremiah 3:1, 3*

And it came to pass through the lightness of her whoredom, that she defiled the land, and committed

Kathe S. Rumsey

adultery [unfaithful to God] with stones [jewels] and with stocks. And yet for all this her treacherous sister Ju'dah hath not turned unto me with her whole heart, but feignedly [in pretense], saith the LORD.

—Jeremiah 3:9–10

And the LORD said unto me, The backsliding Israel hath justified herself more than treacherous Ju'dah. Go and proclaim these words toward the north, and say, Return, thou backsliding Israel, saith the LORD; and I will not cause mine anger to fall upon you: for I am merciful, saith the LORD, and I will not keep anger for ever. Only acknowledge thine iniquity, that thou hast transgressed against the LORD thy God, and hast scattered thy ways to the strangers under every green tree, and ye have not obeyed my voice, saith the LORD. Turn, O backsliding children, saith the LORD; for I am married [rule over] unto you: and I will take you one of a city, and two of a family, and I will bring you to Zion.

—Jeremiah 3:11–14

Church in America

Sow and Reap

One morning while reading Scripture, *Galatians 6:7* caught my attention: "For whatsoever a man soweth, that shall he also reap." The sin of rebellion produced its corrupt fruit that we see manifested in our current culture.

As *baby boomers* growing up during the 1950s and 60s, we experienced a social structure that evolved into something much different from those of our parents and current generations. In America, the *baby boom* phenomenon was unrivaled. Although most were raised in homes that honored God, we became a backsliding generation. God gradually disappeared from homes, schools, government, and every other possible place.

Ironically, a generation that rebelled against their parents' standard of living eventually understood the wisdom of obtaining a college education, living in choice neighborhoods with the best homes and cars. In turn, we are a generation that provided everything imaginable for our own children: an excellent education, travel with enlightening experiences even to foreign destinations, the finest foods, deprived of nothing. There was a sense that opportunities abounded and the whole world was available. Yet many lives remain unfulfilled, even wasted.

> Then said Jesus unto his disciples, Verily I say unto you, That a rich man shall hardly enter into the kingdom of heaven. And again I say unto you, It is easier for a camel to go through the eye of a needle, than for a rich man to enter into the kingdom of God. When his disciples heard it, they were exceedingly amazed, saying, Who then can be saved? But Jesus

beheld them, and said unto them, With men this is
impossible; but with God all things are possible.

—Matthew 19:23–26

A Nation Calls Out to God

In one brief moment—September 11, 2001—our confidence was
shattered. For the first time during my lifetime, the *baby boom*
generation witnessed a catastrophic attack upon American soil,
and innocent lives destroyed. The media broadcasted America's
vulnerability.

Thorns and snares are in the way of the froward
[perverse]: he that doeth keep his soul shall be far
from them. Train up a child in the way he should go:
and when he is old, he will not depart from it.

—Proverbs 22:5–6

Our nation's immediate reaction was a return to God. In
desperation, our godly training from childhood began to emerge
and provide a moral compass in these dark circumstances. Feelings
of patriotism flourished. Political leaders requested prayer for our
nation. Everyone, even the news media, expressed godly terms
of encouragement. Churches experienced an instant population
explosion.

As a nation under assault, 9/11 awakened and humbled us all.
As horrible as it was, this event seemed to bring out the best in
everyone. Initially, people seemed to value our country's godly
heritage and demonstrated an unselfish consciousness toward
one another. However, sadness overwhelmed me when I saw how
quickly our reliance upon God's help and prayer disappeared as
lives returned to normal.

For My people are foolish, they have not known
Me. They are silly children, and they have no
understanding. They are wise to do evil, but to do
good they have no knowledge.

—*Jeremiah 4:22 (NKJV)*

And when thou art spoiled, what wilt thou do? Though
thou clothest thyself with crimson, though thou deckest
thee with ornaments of gold, though thou rentest thy
face with painting, in vain shalt thou make thyself fair;
thy lovers will despise thee, they will seek thy life.

—*Jeremiah 4:30*

And the word of the LORD came unto Zech-a-ri'ah,
saying, Thus speaketh the LORD of hosts, saying,
Execute true judgment, and shew mercy and
compassions every man to his brother: and oppress
not the widow, nor the fatherless, the stranger, nor
the poor; and let none of you imagine evil against his
brother in your heart. But they refused to hearken,
and pulled away the shoulder, and stopped their
ears, that they should not hear. Yea, they made their
hearts as an adamant stone, lest they should hear the
law, and the words which the LORD of hosts hath sent
in his spirit by the former prophets: therefore came
a great wrath from the LORD of hosts.

—*Zechariah 7:8–12*

Light Verses Darkness

Notably, as we headed into the 2008 elections, I sensed tension
escalate in our nation. Wars and more war abroad, fraud, greed,

crime, unemployment, and fiscal uncertainty undermined America's sense of security.

If we foolishly believe our future will improve by the reduction of our carbon footprint, and not by our repentance to God—the Creator of the universe—then we unwisely rely upon the wisdom of man too confidently. What we place before our eyes influences our perception of what we value as worthy or unworthy.

> The light of the body is the eye: if therefore thine eye be single, thy whole body shall be full of light. But if thine eye be evil, thy whole body shall be full of darkness. If therefore the light that is in thee be darkness, how great is that darkness!
>
> *—Matthew 6:22–23*

> Woe unto them that call evil good, and good evil; that put darkness for light, and light for darkness; that put bitter for sweet, and sweet for bitter! Woe unto them that are wise in their own eyes, and prudent in their own sight! Woe unto them that are mighty to drink wine, and men of strength to mingle strong drink: which justify the wicked for reward, and take away the righteousness of the righteous from him! Therefore as the fire devoureth the stubble, and the flame consumeth the chaff, so their root shall be as rottenness, and their blossom shall go up as dust: because they have cast away the law of the Lord of hosts, and despised the word of the Holy One of Israel.
>
> *—Isaiah 5:20–24*

America's Biblical Standard

How perverted has our moral compass become when our culture legalizes crimes against humanity as it preys upon innocent children as well as the elderly? To rationalize such acts of immorality and call such evil good demonstrates the pit of spiritual darkness into which America has plunged. Even so, some politicians have compromised their personal Christian values to maintain their positions of so-called power to be re-elected.

And though they say, The LORD liveth; surely they swear falsely. O LORD, are not thine eyes upon the truth? thou hast stricken them, but they have not grieved; thou hast consumed them, but they have refused to receive correction: they have made their faces harder than a rock; they have refused to return. Therefore I said, Surely these are poor [needy]; they are foolish: for they know not the way of the LORD nor the judgment of their God.

—Jeremiah 5:2–4

Atheists and their legal advocates continue to oppose God and attempt to remove Him and every snippet of His light and truth from American life. As a materialistic society—a nation of idol worshipers—our nation now abides in the complete darkness described in *Matthew 6:23*. God's Word says we are to seek His kingdom and righteousness and the fruit that comes from doing His will. *(Matthew 6:33; Ephesians 5:8–12).*

No man can serve two masters: for either he will hate the one, and love the other; or else he will hold to the one, and despise the other. Ye cannot serve God and mammon.

—*Matthew 6:24*

God's Word tells us that no one can serve both Him and wealth accumulation. In other words, we cannot be a true servant of God and at the same time be in bondage to the things of this world *(1 John 2:15–16).* Merchants spend extravagant amounts of money to persuade customers to purchase their products. Super Bowl ads are a prime example. The unrestrained acquisitions of material goods and indulgence in selfish pleasure have unfortunately become an obsession for many in America. Television programs like *Hoarders* sound an alarm to compulsive practices. Through Satan's deception, life's true principles and an individual's true worth are robbed from the lives of these victims *(Matthew 16:24–26).* God is not a respecter of persons. If He judged Israel for her foolishness, He will judge America for her foolishness. When we obey God, walk in His will, He will meet our needs. He knows what we need before we ask.

Lo, I will bring a nation upon you from far, O house of Israel, saith the LORD; it is a mighty nation, it is an ancient nation, a nation whose language thou knowest not, neither understandest what they say. Their quiver is as an open sepulchre, they are all mighty men.

—*Jeremiah 5:15–16*

I [Paul] know both how to be abased, and I know how to abound: every where and in all things I am instructed both to be full and to be hungry, both to abound and to suffer need. I can do all things through Christ which strengtheneth me.

—Philippians 4:12–13

God Is Our Trustworthy Source

A wonderful and horrible thing is committed in the land; the prophets prophesy falsely, and the priests bear rule by their means; and my people love to have it so: and what will ye do in the end thereof?

—Jeremiah 5:30–31

Led by God's Spirit, we do not need the government or denominations to mandate our financial gifts to others. The poor will always be with us *(Mark 14:7; John 12:8)*. This is not to say we are to be without compassion, but according to Jesus, it is impossible for any government—or non-profits including the church—to eradicate poverty.

Before His death, Jesus went to a house in Bethany. A woman came to the house with an expensive flask of perfumed oil. She poured the oil over Jesus' head. His disciples were indignant by this display, saying, "For this fragrant oil might have been sold for much and given to the poor. But when Jesus was aware of it, He said to them, 'Why do you trouble the woman? For she has done a good work for Me. For you will have the poor with you always, but Me you do not have always. For in pouring this fragrant oil on My body, she did it for My burial. Assuredly, I say to you, wherever this gospel is preached in the whole world, what this woman has done will also be told as a memorial to her'" *(Matthew 26:9–13 NKJV)*.

The good news—the gospel of Jesus Christ—sets captives free! When Peter and John went to the temple to pray, a beggar saw them and asked for alms [gifts of substance or money]. Peter said to him, "Look on us. And he gave heed unto them, expecting to receive something of them. Then Peter said, Silver and gold have I none; but such as I have give I thee: In the name of Jesus Christ of Nazareth rise up and walk" *(Acts 3:4–6).*

What the church needs to offer the poor begins with the Holy Spirit. God's Spirit possesses the power and wisdom to get individuals back on a road of recovery and restoration: spirit, mind, and body. Since God provides for all His children, the church would be far more effective to help others through intercessory prayer in the Holy Spirit, and then obey His wise directions to meet their needs.

Government and all its assistance programs only scratch the surface toward true recovery. At best, they are temporary solutions to deep-rooted problems. Though their intentions appear worthwhile, worldly programs sometimes compound society's problems, forcing people into deeper bondage. We need God to be God in our lives and the lives of others. Only our Maker knows what is necessary to bring genuine change and restoration into an individual's life.

Confess Jesus Before Others

And fear not them which kill the body, but are not able to kill the soul: but rather fear him which is able to destroy both soul and body in hell. Are not two sparrows sold for a farthing? and one of them shall not fall on the ground without your Father. But the very hairs of your head are all numbered. Fear ye not therefore, ye are of more value than many sparrows. Whosoever therefore shall confess me [Jesus] before men, him will I confess also before my Father which is in heaven. But whosoever shall deny me before men, him will I also deny before my Father which is in heaven.

—*Matthew 10:28–33*

Rebellion Danced Her Way into the Heart of a Nation
As a volunteer for various organizations, I became aware of gross abuses perpetrated upon the weak and frail in our society. In prayer, these thoughts came to me and I would like to share them from what I consider an historical perspective.

In the late 1960's, the "free love" movement invaded our society, coupled with illegal drug abuse. "Dropping out and turning on" echoed from coast to coast. Looking back, I now view this as a turning point of a generation that called darkness light. There were the "love children," "peace signs," "the age of Aquarius." The music was alluring. "Flower power" made everything joyful and seemingly innocent. Was it really?

Public behaviors once considered unspeakable became acceptable. The culture redefined social defiance as freethinkers of non-repression. What could be so wrong with being the "love children?" Yet these were tumultuous times for our nation. Where was the church while all of this was happening? I remember when the church I attended began to offer *folk* services. Music and fashions defined the budding culture around us. It seemed comforting at first, but now I ask myself, why? Adaptation to the times made the world around us seem less threatening, friendlier, and more acceptable.

Church denominations adjusted to the changing times. No one seemed to recognize the shift in our moral compass. The body of Christ lacked godly wisdom to stand and resist this wave of seduction. Compromise by nature is more comforting than confrontation. Our nation and the church fell into relaxed acceptance of darkness through music, drugs, and rebellion; our moral perception adapted with the gradual changes of society.

Be not deceived; God is not mocked: for whatsoever a man soweth, that shall he will also reap. For he that soweth to his flesh shall of the flesh reap corruption; but he that soweth to the Spirit shall of the Spirit reap life everlasting.

—*Galatians 6:7–8*

I believe the fruit of what we witness currently in America and in the church result from seeds sown fifty-plus years ago. While the church joined forces with the world and failed to humble herself, pray, repent from her evil ways, and seek God's presence, our country lost her way. The church effortlessly compromised and conformed to the world's ways. Worldly programs became the catalyst for drawing attendees into church pews.

Surely, the late 1960s and early 70s were a time of turmoil. The *boomer* generation had sown the seeds of rebellion *(1 Samuel 15:23)*. Self-interest, drugs, and free love plowed the deep of America's soul and multifaceted sin took root. The conceit of our own wisdom blinded us as a nation and church as we turned from God's righteousness. We replaced His righteousness with our own self-righteous ethics with every so-called god or none at all.

This know also, that in the last days perilous times shall come. For men shall be lovers of their own selves, covetous, boasters, proud, blasphemers, disobedient to parents, unthankful, unholy, without natural affection, trucebreakers, false accusers, incontinent, fierce, despisers of those that are good, traitors, heady, highminded, lovers of pleasures more than lovers of God; having a form of godliness, but denying the power thereof: from such turn away. Ever learning, and never able to come to the knowledge of the truth.

—*2 Timothy 3:1–5, 7*

Woe to you, scribes and Pharisees, hypocrites! For ye devour widows' houses, and for pretense make long prayer: therefore ye shall receive the greater damnation.

—*Matthew 23:14*

The Snoring Church

The body of Christ must wake up and pray. The church has been spiritually asleep producing only dissonant noises. Yet Jesus is faithful. He remains the same yesterday, today, and forever. He is quick to forgive when we repent and is abundantly generous with His mercy and grace. His love for us is greater than our sin.

Therefore also now, saith the LORD, Turn ye even to me with all of your heart, and with fasting, and with weeping, and with mourning: and rend your heart, and not your garments, and turn unto the LORD your God: for he is gracious and merciful, slow to anger, and of great kindness, and repenteth him of the evil.

—*Joel 2:12–13*

Society Changes, God Does Not

Americans sense the helplessness and frailty of life as we know it. God have mercy. He did not intend for man to live in habitual sin, separated from Him forever. Daily—through personal choice—both America and the church pronounce their own demise through their own free will. God, however, never changes.

> Therefore thou shalt speak all these words unto them; but they will not hearken to thee: thou shalt also call unto them; but they will not answer thee. But thou shalt say unto them, This is a nation that obeyeth not the voice of the Lord their God, nor receiveth correction; truth is perished, and is cut off from their mouth.
>
> —*Jeremiah 7:27–28*

Individually as Christians, we must humble ourselves and return to God if we hope to see Him restore our nation. America is not perfect. The church is not perfect. Mankind is not perfect. But if we are to serve a perfect God, then we must know what His Word says and be obedient to it.

> Therefore whosoever heareth these sayings of mine, and doeth them, I will liken him unto a wise man, which built his house on the rock: and the rain descended, and the floods came, and the winds blew, and beat upon that house; and it fell not: for it was founded upon a rock. And every one that heareth these sayings of mine, and doeth them not, shall be likened unto a foolish man, which built his house upon the sand: and the rain descended, and the floods came, and the winds blew, and beat upon that house; and it fell: and great was the fall of it.
>
> —*Matthew 7:24–27*

Fervent Prayer

Overcome the World

Jesus paid the price for all of humanity's sins at Calvary. He has overcome the world. We, too, can overcome. "For whatsoever is born of God overcometh the world: and this is the victory that overcometh the world, even our faith. Who is he that overcometh the world, but he that believeth that Jesus is the Son of God?" *(1 John 5:4–5)*. If we call ourselves Christians, we must be doers of God's Word, not just hearers. Therein rests the difference between our victory or defeat.

> Stand in the gate of the Lord's house, and proclaim there this word, and say, Hear the word of the Lord, all ye of Ju'dah, that enter in at these gates to worship the Lord. Thus saith the Lord of hosts, the God of Israel. Amend your ways and your doings, and I will cause you to dwell in this place. Trust ye not in lying words, saying, The temple of the Lord, The temple of the Lord, The temple of the Lord, are these. For if ye thoroughly amend your ways and your doings; if ye thoroughly execute judgment between a man and his neighbour; if ye oppress not the stranger, the fatherless, and the widow, and shed not innocent blood in this place, neither walk after other gods to your hurt: then will I cause you to dwell in this place, in the land that I gave to your fathers, for ever and ever.
>
> *—Jeremiah 7:2–7*

God's Word is explicit. We must repent and turn from our wicked ways and seek His presence *(2 Chronicles 7:14; James 4:8)*. The church must be the house of prayer. Spiritual warfare is not effortless; but America's future desperately depends upon God's grace and intervention.

People everywhere sense we live in perilous times. The church for which Jesus Christ died must wake up and pray. We must invite God back into our lives. We must put God first and learn to love one another even as He loves us. Only the truth from the Word of God will expose and silence the lies of the Devil, the author of confusion.

America's fruit of rebellion is ever before our eyes. The *free love* movement of the 1960s and 70s eventually reaped a bountiful crop of pornography, sexual perversion, human sex trafficking, assaults on seniors in some extended care facilities, and even sexual exploits upon some with cogitative disabilities. A harvest of moral decay has permeated the lives of young and old alike.

Marijuana and drug experimentations of the 1960s and 70s have opened the door to extensive acceptance of drug usage. Even the consumption of prescription drugs among people of all ages is unprecedented. Some state legislators have brought to the table of debate the legalization of marijuana for the general public's usage under the guise of medicinal need. However, for government, it is just another source of tax revenue and lack of concern for its citizenry.

Some facilities originally created for the care of aging populations currently house dysfunctional drug addicts alongside our senior citizens. Tragically, many of these facilities have become unbearable workplaces for staff members and a nightmare for fragile residents.

His Church's Responsibility

In America, our culture for the most part no longer honors, cherishes, nor protects our aging citizens. What should be the role of the church? What could we as individual believers do to make life more meaningful for the elderly in light of eternity? Have we conveniently overlooked those considered no longer a viable part of our communities? How many of our elderly enter assisted living facilities without a personal relationship with God? How many enter nursing homes only to fall victim to over-medication, rendering them docile and unresponsive? Yet, some remain unprepared for life after death. What is the church's accountability to God and the elderly who are on their final walk through their earthly existence?

When I see the church neglect widows and hear "The youth are the future of the church," I am saddened. Are we here to recruit new members and to use our youth to sustain broken down religious systems, denominations, doctrines of men and all that is irrelevant to the kingdom of God? If so, the church remains indistinguishable from the world. We must not sacrifice the future of the younger generations for selfish gain, while allowing the elderly to slip through the cracks of society into eternity unprepared.

What is the church's true calling? Yes, it is important to train up the youth, but not at the expense of even one of our elderly dying without Christ. Our young people sense the hypocrisy within the church. Actions speak to them louder than words. It is not God's will that anyone be destined to eternal separation from Him unnecessarily *(John 3:16)*.

And if Christ be not risen, then is our preaching vain, and your faith is also vain. Yea, and we are found false witnesses of God; because we have testified of God that he raised up Christ: whom he raised not up, if so be that the dead rise not. For if the dead rise not, then is not Christ raised: and if Christ is not raised, your faith is vain; ye are yet in your sins.

—1 Corinthians 15:14–17

Hour to Watch and Pray

The choice to restore America lies in the hands of the church. This is the hour to watch and pray. Jesus said His house is "the house of prayer" *(Matthew 21:13; Mark 11:17; Luke 19:46)*. How we utilize our time is a choice we make every day. As the body of Christ, we cannot allow the cares, pleasures, or riches of this world to choke His Word. It is time for the church to bear godly fruit. Individually and corporately, the restoration America desperately needs will begin with change within the heart of each one of us.

We need God's hand of mercy extended to His church in order to heal our brokenness *(Daniel 9:17–19)*. Let us turn our eyes to Him. God does not desire for America—founded upon His biblical principles—to remain in the hands of His spiritual enemies *(Ephesians 6:12)*.

In genuine unconditional love, let us pray and help one another to stand firm and be strong in our resistance against the tidal wave of debauchery. *In God We Trust* must become more than an American motto inscribed on our currency. These words must become a living reality in our nation.

What shall we say then? Shall we continue in sin that grace may abound? Certainly not! How shall we who died to sin live any longer in it? Or do you not know that as many of us as were baptized into Christ Jesus were baptized into His death? Therefore we were buried with Him through baptism into death, that just as Christ was raised from the dead by the glory of the Father, even so we also should walk in newness of life. For if we have been united together in the likeness of His death, certainly we also shall be in the likeness of His resurrection, knowing this, that our old man was crucified with Him, that the body of sin might be done away with, that we should no longer be slaves of sin. For he who has died has been freed from sin. Now if we died with Christ, we believe that we shall also live with Him, knowing that Christ, having been raised from the dead, dies no more. Death no longer has dominion over Him. For the death that He died, He died to sin once for all; but the life that He lives, He lives to God. Likewise, you also, reckon yourselves to be dead indeed to sin, but alive to God in Christ Jesus our Lord. Therefore do not let sin reign in your mortal body, that you should obey it in its lusts.

—*Romans 6:1–12 (NKJV)*

As twenty-first century citizens of the United States of America, we have reaped blessings from God that no other nation in the world has experienced. Our forefathers fought and died for true freedom from tyranny. They determined in their hearts to honor and serve God foremost.

When we share in the fruit of our ancestors' obedience and what they determined in their hearts to accomplish, the church must question the effectiveness of her present-day testimony. We are to be salt and light *(Matthew 5:13; Mark 9:50; Luke 14:34–35)*.

Wake up, church. Now is the time for every Christian to make a difference. Pray and ask God what He would have you do. Born

Kathe S. Rumsey

again Christians, the body of Christ on earth, have the authority Jesus provides through the Holy Spirit. Prayer releases Jesus' power on earth and in heaven. Each one of us has a specific job. We must occupy until Jesus returns *(Luke 19:13)*.

And Jesus knew their thoughts, and said unto them, Every kingdom divided against itself is brought to desolation; and every city or house divided against itself shall not stand.

—Matthew 12:25

Now we exhort you, brethren, warn them that are unruly, comfort the feebleminded, support the weak, be patient toward all men. See that none render evil for evil unto any man; but ever follow that which is good, both among yourselves, and to all men. Rejoice evermore, pray without ceasing. In every thing give thanks: for this is the will of God in Christ Jesus concerning you. Quench not the Spirit. Despise not prophesyings. Prove all things; hold fast that which is good. Abstain from all appearance of evil.

—1 Thessalonians 5:14–22

God be merciful unto us, and bless us; and cause his face to shine upon us; Se'lah. That thy way may be known upon earth, thy saving health among all nations. Let the peoples praise thee, O God; Let all the people praise thee. O let the nations be glad and sing for joy: for thou shalt judge the people righteously, and govern the nations upon earth. Se'lah. Let the people praise thee, O God; let all the people praise thee. Then shall the earth yield her increase; and God, even our own God, shall bless us; and all the ends of the earth shall fear him.

—Psalm 67:1–7

Christians in America must once again be salt and light to those near us, and to those around the world. We must put aside our differences within the body of Christ. For the church—founded by Jesus Christ to function—we must submit to Jesus as head in everything *(Ephesians 1:22)*. No man or denomination can take Jesus' place.

If "All scripture is given by inspiration of God, and is profitable for doctrine, for reproof, for correction, for instruction in righteousness" then mankind cannot ignore it, forget it or change God's Word just to make ourselves more comfortable in sin *(2 Timothy 3:16–17)*. God is the Creator of all mankind, the heavens, and the earth, all that is seen and unseen. God ordained a plan, and His plan will be fulfilled whether men believe that He is the Creator or not *(Colossians 1:15–23)*.

For unto us a child is born, unto us a son is given: and the government shall be upon his shoulder; and his name shall be called Wonderful, Counsellor, The mighty God, The everlasting Father, The Prince of Peace. Of the increase of his government and peace there shall be no end, upon the throne of David, and upon his kingdom, to order it, and to establish it with judgment and with justice from henceforth even for ever. The zeal of the LORD of hosts will perform this.

—Isaiah 9:6–7

Transformation

Pray and Seek God

> If my people, which are called by my name, shall
> humble themselves, and pray, and seek my face, and
> turn from their wicked ways; then will I hear from
> heaven, and will forgive their sin, and heal their land.
>
> —*2 Chronicles 7:14*

It does not matter how complex America's problems seem; our God is mightier. America's founders' God is the same God we must seek and serve. He is the God of the impossible *(Matthew 19:26)*. It is time for the church, the body of Christ, to be responsible— unite—and fervently pray for our nation *(James 5:16)*.

If we seek God's wisdom, the Holy Spirit will reveal the knowledge needed to win spiritual battles for our nation and ourselves *(Matthew 4:4)*. God's prayer warriors must put on the whole armor of God *(Ephesians 6:10–18)*. We must be filled with the same Spirit of truth that filled Jesus. The power of God and His Word in us are greater than any obstacle that stands in the way of His promises. Without God, we cannot defeat any hindrance in our life.

> What shall we then say to these things? If God be for
> us, who can be against us? Nay, in all these things
> we are more than conquerors through him that loved
> us. For I am persuaded, that neither death, nor life,
> nor angels, nor principalities, nor powers, nor things
> present, nor things to come, nor height, nor depth,
> nor any other creature, shall be able to separate us

from the love of God, which is in Christ Jesus our Lord.

—*Romans 8:31, 37–39*

And you He made alive, who were dead in trespasses and sins, in which you once walked according to the course of this world, according to the prince of the power of the air, the spirit who now works in the sons of disobedience, among whom also we all once conducted ourselves in the lusts of our flesh, fulfilling the desires of the flesh and of the mind, and were by nature children of wrath, just as the others.

But God, who is rich in mercy, because of His great love with which He loved us, even when we were dead in trespasses, made us alive together with Christ (by grace you have been saved), and raised us up together, and made us sit together in the heavenly places in Christ Jesus, that in the ages to come He might show the exceeding riches of His grace in His kindness toward us in Christ Jesus. For by grace you have been saved through faith, and that not of yourselves; it is the gift of God, not of works, lest anyone should boast. For we are His workmanship, created in Christ Jesus for good works, which God prepared beforehand that we should walk in them.

—*Ephesians 2:1–10 (NKJV)*

That he [Jesus] might present it to himself a glorious church, not having spot, or wrinkle, or any such thing; but that it should be holy and without blemish.

—*Ephesians 5:27*

Kathe S. Rumsey

It is not too late for the church to get herself right with God. The body of Christ must wake up. Our God is more powerful than anything we face as individuals, as the church, and as a nation. This is not the hour for defeat, or retreat. God is the help we need to restore our nation to her godly heritage. Spiritually, we must be courageous and take back territory for God's kingdom.

> Then he answered and spake unto me, saying, This is the word of the LORD to Ze-rub'ba-bel, saying, Not by might, nor by power, but by my spirit, saith the LORD of hosts. Who art thou O great mountain? before Ze-rub'ba-bel thou shalt become a plain: and he shall bring forth the headstone thereof with shoutings, crying, Grace, grace unto it. Moreover the word of the LORD came unto me, saying, The hands of Ze-rub'ba-bel have laid the foundation of this house; his hands shall also finish it; and thou shalt know that the LORD of hosts hath sent me unto you. For who hath despised the day of small things? for they shall rejoice, and shall see the plummet in the hand of Ze-rub'ba-bel with those seven; they are the eyes of the LORD, which run to and fro through the whole earth.
>
> —*Zechariah 4:6–10*

The church must return to her first love, Jesus Christ *(Revelation 2:4)*. Ask Him how He would have you spend your next twenty-four hours *(Revelation 2:1–7)*. One by one, each of us must seek God with all our heart. May God once again bless America. At a time when Americans put their hope in God, the greatest witness to God's sovereign power is for the world to see America restored to the great nation she once was.

I BESEECH you therefore, brethren, by the mercies of God, that ye present your bodies a living sacrifice, holy, acceptable unto God, which is your reasonable service. And be not conformed to this world: but be ye transformed by the renewing of your mind, that ye may prove what is that good, and acceptable, and perfect, will of God.

—Romans 12:1–2

Power Filled Church

In His Power

> Humble yourselves therefore under the mighty hand of God, that he may exalt you in due time: casting all your care upon him; for he careth for you. Be sober, be vigilant; because your adversary the devil, as a roaring lion, walketh about, seeking whom he may devour: whom resist steadfast in the faith, knowing that the same afflictions are accomplished in your brethren that are in the world. But the God of all grace, who hath called us unto his eternal glory by Christ Jesus, after that ye have suffered a while, make you perfect, stablish, strengthen, settle you. To him be glory and dominion for ever and ever. Amen.
>
> *—1 Peter 5: 6–11*

If church leaders do not first humble themselves, how will they set the example for their congregations? Each member of the body of Christ must have ears to hear the Holy Spirit and submit to Christ as head in everything *(Ephesians 5:23–24).*

God Sends the Holy Spirit

Peter stood with the other eleven disciples on the day of Pentecost and said, "For these are not drunken, as ye suppose, seeing it is but the third hour of the day. But this is that which was spoken by the prophet Jo'el; and it shall come to pass in the last days, saith God, I will pour out of my Spirit upon all flesh: and your sons and your daughters shall prophesy, your young men shall see visions, and your old men shall dream dreams: and on my servants and on my handmaidens I will pour out in those days of my Spirit; and they shall prophesy" *(Acts 2:15–18)*.

Two important things to note from *Acts 2:15–18*, "It shall come to pass in the last days," and "I will pour out of my Spirit upon all flesh." Many Christians refer to the "last days" as the days just before the rapture of the bride, but we see from this verse that the last days began at Pentecost. We also see that God began to pour out of His Spirit. Some denominations teach that the outpouring of the Holy Spirit was an isolated historical event and no longer occurs. In truth, these are the last days and Jesus continues to baptize with the Holy Spirit to all who will receive Him *(Mark 1:7–8; Luke 11:13; John 7:37)*.

If the church is to bear fruit, she must abide in the Word and submit to God's Holy Spirit in everything. The Spirit of truth must lead and teach Jesus' church. For too long, pastors and priests have taught and led congregations by their seminary educations. In most cases, every wind of doctrine that blows through the halls of theological institutions influence current instruction and business models that bring division in the body of Christ *(Ephesians 4:13–15)*. Believers must have ears to hear the Holy Spirit of God *(Revelation 2:1–3:22)*.

Time for Godly Action
How would I prioritize my time if it were my final day on earth, a family member's final day on earth, an elderly friend's last day on earth, my neighbor's final day on earth? What if I came upon an accident victim dying, what would I do? What is my responsibility to America who has veered from her godly heritage? Daily intercessory prayer carries significance and power. From Scripture we know prayer—based upon mustard seed-sized faith—will move mountains.

America once represented the light on a hill, a beacon of hope to the world. What price is the church willing to pay to restore godliness in America? Jesus considered all humankind worth the sacrifice He paid at Calvary. We must not waste another moment. God has plans for this nation just as He has plans for us as individuals.

The church in America must not surrender to her spiritual enemy. We must not retreat, while blaming government and others for the demise of our nation. We must be the Spirit-filled force in America that occupies until Jesus returns *(Luke 19:13)*. God loves His children too much to ignore our sinful ways *(Hebrews 12:6)*.

Isaiah 56:7, Matthew 21:13, Mark 11:17, Luke 19:46 sound the wakeup call to all: "My house shall be called the house of prayer." Let us awake from our slumber, pray, and seek God's plan for our lives, then immediately put His plan into action. Jesus asked His followers to watch and pray with Him for one hour.

How often have we desired to pray yet the distractions and cares of this life prevent us from remaining focused? God's ways truly are not our ways. It is easy to hate our enemies until we come face to face with *Ephesians 6:12*. When we truly understand this verse, we will see the spiritual realm in operation and how it influences the actions of others. Some have become pawns in the hands of the evil forces of this age. The enemy— the Accuser— attempts to manipulate our thoughts and actions to carry out his schemes. Rejoice. By God's grace, believers are no longer subject to the bondage of the enemy *(John 8:36)*.

Watch and pray, that ye enter not into temptation: The spirit indeed is willing, but the flesh is weak.

—*Matthew 26:41*

You have heard that it was said, You shall love your neighbor and hate your enemy. But I [Jesus] say to you, love your enemies, bless those who curse you, do good to those who hate you, and pray for those who spitefully use you and persecute you, that you may be sons of your Father in heaven; for He makes His sun rise on the evil and on the good, and sends rain on the just and on the unjust. For if you love those who love you, what reward have you? Do not even the tax collectors do the same?

—*Matthew 5:43–46 (NKJV)*

Wherefore he saith, Awake thou that sleepest, and arise from the dead, and Christ shall give thee light.

—*Ephesians 5:14*

Blow ye the trumpet in Zion, and sound an alarm in my holy mountain: let all the inhabitants of the land tremble: for the day of the LORD cometh, for is nigh at hand.

—*Joel 2:1*

If this book inspires you to pursue God with renewed passion, I pray you will share what you have learned with others.

Small Group Study

1. Why does the _____ of the gospel of Jesus Christ and the kingdom of ___ remain a mystery to most church members?

2. What has lulled our nation and the _____ to sleep, camouflaging ungodly influences?

3. Through _____ and the _____ of the church, America's future does not have to remain in a downward spiral *(Jeremiah 29:11; James 5:17–18)*.

4. The weeping prophet, _____, struggled emotionally within his prophetic office because of a rebellious nation that walked in debauchery and rejected his message to repent of their evil ways.

5. When we attempt to remedy our nation's present-day problems with situational ethics, thereby sugarcoating sin, spirits of _____ operate unrestrained? *(1 John 2:18–21)*.

6. Church members must reject man-made programs that mirror the world's _____ just to increase church attendance.

7. Why must Christians not buy into the slick marketing programs offered by _____ who are disguised in sheep's clothing within the church? *(John 10:12; 1 Corinthians 2:1–13)*.

8. What is the promise of God the Father that will dramatically change anyone's prayer life? God is no respecter of persons. If believers desire to have this gift, our heavenly Father will give

the _____ _____ to those who ask (*Mark 16:17; Luke 11:13; Acts 10:44–46; 19:6; 1 Corinthians 12:10–11, 27–28*).

9. America's churches of all denominations consistently raise finances to send and support their _____ around the world. Yet, many fail to feed the flock at home, robbing congregations of their spiritual sustenance. Explain.

10. God's abundant wisdom is available to His church to correct the enormous problems that erode America's foundation. Through the _____ of believers, God has granted His people the keys of authority both in heaven and on earth. Jesus admonishes us to pray; He named His church "the house of prayer" *(Matthew 21:13)*.

11. Outward appearances must not deceive the body of Christ. Some churches may appear strong and prosperous, but remember Jesus cursed the ____ _____ because it produced no fruit *(Matthew 21:19–22)*.

12. Although most were raised in homes that honored God, we became a _____ generation, God gradually disappeared from homes, schools, government, and every other possible place. What has resulted?

13. After the 9/11 attack on America, people's immediate reaction was to return to _____. In desperation, our godly training from childhood began to emerge and provide a moral compass in these dark circumstances. Feelings of patriotism flourished. Political leaders requested prayer for our nation. Everyone, even the news media, expressed godly terms of

encouragement. Churches experienced an instant population explosion. What happened when people's fears subsided?

14. Atheists and their legal advocates continue to oppose _____ and attempt to remove Him, and every snippet of His light and truth from American life. As a materialistic society, a nation of idol worshipers, do we presently abide in complete darkness of *Matthew 6:23*?

15. I remember when the church I attended began to offer *folk* services. Music and fashions defined the budding culture around us. It seemed _____ at first, but now I ask myself, why? Adaptation to the times made the world around us seem less threatening, friendlier, and more _____. What has been the fruit it produced?

16. The body of Christ must wake up and pray. The church has been spiritually _____ producing dissonant noises. Yet Jesus is faithful. He remains the same yesterday, _____ and forever. He is quick to forgive when we repent and is abundantly generous with His mercy and grace.

17. Individually as Christians, we must _____ ourselves and return to God if we hope to see Him restore our nation. America is not _____. The church is not _____. Mankind is not _____. But if we are to serve a _____ God, then we must know what His Word says and be obedient to it.

18. God's Word is explicit. We must _____ and turn from our wicked ways and seek His presence *(2 Chronicles 7:14)*. The church must be the house of _____. Spiritual warfare is not

effortless, but America's future depends upon God's _____ and intervention.

19. America's fruit of _____ is ever before our eyes. The "free love" of the 1960s reaped a bountiful crop of pornography, _____, human sex trafficking, assaults on seniors in some extended care facilities, and even sexual exploits upon some with cogitative disabilities. A harvest of moral decay has permeated the lives of young and old alike.

20. Some state legislators have brought to the table of debate the _____ of marijuana for the general public's usage under the guise of medicinal need. However, for government it is just another source of tax revenue and lack of _____ for their citizenry.

21. In America, our culture for the most part no longer honors, cherishes, nor _____ our aging citizens. What should be the role of the church? What could we as individual believers do to make life more meaningful for the elderly in light of eternity? How many die needlessly without Jesus as their Lord and Savior in nursing homes?

22. Our young people sense the hypocrisy within the church. Actions speak to them louder than _____. It is not God's will that anyone be destined to eternal separation from Him unnecessarily *(John 3:16)*.

23. The choice to restore America lies in the hands of the church. This is the hour to watch and pray. Jesus said His house is "the house of prayer" *(Matthew 21:13; Mark 11:17; Luke 19:46)*.

How we utilize our _____ is a choice we make every day. As the body of Christ, we cannot allow the cares, pleasures, or riches of this _____ to choke His Word. It is time for the church to bear godly fruit. Individually and corporately, the restoration America desperately needs will begin with change within the heart of each one of us.

24. In genuine _____ love, let us pray and _____ one another to stand firm and be strong in our resistance against the tidal wave of debauchery. *In God We Trust* must become more than an American motto inscribed on our currency. These words must become a living reality in our country.

25. As twenty-first century citizens of the United States of America, we have reaped blessings from God that no other _____ in the world has experienced. Our forefathers fought and died for true freedom from tyranny. They determined in their hearts to honor and _____ God foremost.

26. Wake up, church! Now is the _____ for every Christian to make a difference. Pray and ask God what He would have you do. Born-again Christians, the body of Christ on earth, have the authority Jesus provides through the Holy Spirit. Prayer releases Jesus' power on earth and in _____. Each one of us has a specific job. We must occupy until Jesus returns *(Luke 19:13)*.

27. Christians in America must once again be salt and light to those around us and to those around the world. We must put aside our differences within the body of Christ. For the

_____ founded by Jesus Christ to function, we must submit to Jesus as _____ *(Ephesians 1:22)*

28. It does not matter how _____ America's problems seem; our God is mightier. Our founders' God is the same God we must seek and serve today. He is the God of the impossible *(Matthew 19:26)*. It is time for the church, the body of Christ, to be responsible, unite, and fervently pray for our nation *(James 5:16)*.

29. It is not too late for the church to get herself _____ with God. The body of Christ must wake up. Our God is more powerful than _____ we face as individuals, as the church, and as a nation. This is not the hour for defeat or to retreat. God is the _____ we need to restore our nation to her godly heritage. Spiritually, we must be courageous and take back territory for God's kingdom.

30. The church must _____ to her first love, Jesus Christ *(Revelation 2:4)*. Ask Him how He would have you spend your next twenty-four hours *(Revelation 2:1–7)*. One by one, each of ____ must seek God with all our heart. May God once again bless America.

31. If church leaders do not first humble themselves, how will they set the _____ for their congregations? The body of Christ must have _____ to hear the Holy Spirit and _____ to Christ as head in everything *(Ephesians 5:23–24)*.

32. Two important things to note from *Acts 2:15–18,* "It shall come to pass in the last days," and "I will pour out of my Spirit

upon all flesh." Many Christians refer to the *last days* as the days just before the rapture of the bride, but we see from this verse that the last days _____ at Pentecost. We also see that God began to pour out of His Spirit. Some _____ teach that the outpouring of the Holy Spirit was an isolated historical event and no longer occurs. In truth, these are the last days, and God continues to give the gift of the Holy Spirit to all who will receive Him *(Mark 1:7–8; Luke 11:13; John 7:37)*.

33. How would we prioritize our _____ if it were our final day on earth, a family member's final day, an elderly friend's last day, my neighbor's final day on earth? What if we came upon an accident victim dying, what would we do? What is the church's responsibility to our homeland? The USA has veered from her godly heritage. Daily intercessory prayer carries significance and power.

34. From Scripture, we know prayer—based upon mustard seed-sized faith—will move mountains. America once represented the light on a _____, a beacon of hope to the world. What _____ is the church willing to pay to restore godliness in America? Jesus considered all humankind worth the sacrifice He paid at Calvary. We must not waste another moment. God has plans for this nation just as He has _____ for us as individuals.

35. It is easy to hate our enemies until we come face to face with *Ephesians 6:12*. When we truly understand this verse, we will see the spiritual realm in operation and how it _____ the actions of others.

A Soldier's Journal

God's Army Bible Boot Camp – Day 1

Am I committed to the rigorous preparation needed to take me to the next level of training in God's Word? Am I prepared to serve God Almighty without compromise? What has brought me to this point in my life? As a believer, what is my overall spiritual fitness level? Did God draft me into His service, or did I voluntarily come to this decision to serve Him? As a soldier in God's army, I must take my orders from my Commander-in-Chief, Jesus Christ, without questioning His tactics.

> And the LORD shall utter his voice before his army: for his camp is very great: for he is strong that executeth his word.
>
> —*Joel 2:11.*

There are essential lessons to be learned by every person who commits to serving in God's army. It is critical for me to understand basic training is not only for my protection, but also for the protection of others.

What fundamentals are required of God's prayer warrior to prepare to overcome the enemy? It is imperative for me to be prepared and to serve alongside other equipped believers in God's army. The Bible is my training manual. The Holy Spirit is my Drill Sergeant. God desires the best training possible for me and the body of Christ. We are to occupy territory until Jesus returns.

Kathe S. Rumsey

God's Army Bible Boot Camp – Day 2

Enlisted service personnel who have attended military boot camp understand that most recruits begin boot camp among strangers. Many have little knowledge of how to handle military weaponry; and if sent out without proper training, they would be overcome by the enemy. These trainees learn the importance of following orders and to rely upon fellow soldiers' expertise. The troops must learn how to work together as a unit.

For the past 35 years, I have met weekly with my prayer partner, trustworthy friend, to study the Word of God and to pray. Under the direction of the Holy Spirit, we found Scripture verses to stand on in prayer for our needs and those of others. God has been faithful in answering our prayers in ways that astonish both of us and keep us motivated. It is my desire in warfare training to be equipped, ready to help others who come face to face with our common enemy. God's Word is the key to our victories.

I do not have all the answers to life's challenges. The more I learn from God's Word, the more I realize I know so little. God's provisions and victories are available for all who come to Him in faith. I trust the Holy Spirit as my Drill Sergeant—the Spirit of truth—who guides me into all truth.

> If ye abide in me, and my words [rhema] abide in you, ye shall ask what ye will, and it shall be done unto you. Herein is my Father is glorified, that ye bear much fruit; so shall ye be my disciples. As the

Father hath loved me, so have I loved you: continue
ye in my love.

—*John 15:7–9*

The more I abide in God's Word and Jesus' commands, the
better trained I will be as a soldier in the Lord's army.

God's Army Bible Boot Camp – Day 3

> Proclaim ye this among the Gentiles; Prepare war,
> wake up the mighty men, let all the men of war draw
> near; let them come up; beat your plowshares into
> swords, and your pruninghooks into spears; let the
> weak say, I am strong. Assemble yourselves, and
> come, all ye heathen, and gather yourselves together
> round about: thither cause thy mighty ones to come
> down, O LORD.
>
> *—Joel 3:9–11*

By the time one arrives for Boot Camp, they have made up their mind that they may come face to face with combatant forces. This requires readiness training. *Ephesians 6:10–11* says, "Finally, my brethren be strong in the Lord, and in the power of his might. Put on the whole armour of God, that ye may be able to stand against the wiles of the devil."

The Bible does not say I must put on the whole armor so that I can stand against the wiles of men. "For we wrestle not against flesh and blood, but against principalities, against powers, against the rulers of the darkness of this world, against spiritual wickedness in high places. Wherefore take unto you the whole armour of God, that ye may be able to withstand in the evil day, and having done all, to stand" *(Ephesians 6:12–13)*.

God has given us the Spirit of truth, not the spirit of fear *(2 Timothy 1:7)*. I must have ears to hear what the Holy Spirit is saying to me—Jesus' church—if I wish to serve My Lord and Savior. It is important that I understand the basics of spiritual warfare, not only to protect myself, but also to protect others.

What do I need to know as a spiritual warrior in God's army to overcome?

Jesus' church is here to help one another mature and become effective prayer warriors in the army of God. United, we stand firm and occupy territory until Jesus returns.

God's Army Bible Boot Camp – Day 4

Our enemy, Satan, is real and very cunning. However, he has limited recruits on his side. As a born-again believer in Jesus Christ, I have God the Father—God the Son—and God the Holy Spirit—in addition to God's angelic army on my side.

Prayer based upon faith is the major key to victory. No matter what I encounter, my circumstances have not taken God by surprise. Jesus tells me to be courageous because He has overcome the world *(John 16:33)*.

Here I am on day 4 of Bible Boot Camp declaring, I AM STRONG! I AM A VICTORIOUS OVERCOMER! In Christ, I have what it takes to overcome.

> For though we walk in the flesh, we do not war after the flesh: (For the weapons of our warfare are not carnal, but mighty through God to the pulling down strongholds;) casting down imaginations, and every high thing that exalteth itself against the knowledge of God, and bringing into captivity every thought to the obedience of Christ; and having in a readiness to revenge all disobedience, when your obedience is fulfilled.
>
> *—2 Corinthians 10:3–6*

Boldly I proclaim, I AM STRONG, yes sir! I AM STRONG! *(Joel 3:10)*. Boot Camp is all about tactical training and obedience to orders. As a soldier of Christ, I must decide to be obedient to His commands no matter what happens in my life. It does not matter what I think, or how I feel. The only thing that matters is what my Commander-in-Chief, Jesus Christ, has commanded.

My Drill Sergeant, the Holy Spirit goes by the Book. He will not deviate from commands just because I am tired or think I do not need the required training. I must learn to accurately identify my enemy *(Ephesians 6:12)*.

God's Army Bible Boot Camp – Day 5

> The Warrior is someone who says, This is my family.
> This is my country. This is my faith. And this is what
> threatens it. This is the enemy. You will not hurt what
> I hold dear. You will not hurt what I love without
> coming through me.
>
> *—General Jerry Boykin*

The most effective Christians in God's kingdom are prayer warriors. Intercessors defeat the enemy—the devil's kingdom—here on earth. As one of God's intercessors, I must not enter battle without the whole armor of God *(Ephesians 6:10–18)*.

> Wherefore take unto you the whole armour of God,
> that ye may be able to withstand in the evil day, and
> having done all, to stand. Stand therefore, having
> your loins girt about with truth, and having on the
> breastplate of righteousness.
>
> *—Ephesians 6:13–14*

My first battle-ready defense is to measure the ethical standards of our world by the truth of God's Word. Satan has released an all-out assault on the moral compass guiding our lives. It is only when I submit to the truth of Scripture that I am protected. God's Word has not changed. When man chooses to legalize sin, it does not annul the consequences sin produces.

As a faithful soldier, I am learning to do exactly what my Commander-in-Chief, Jesus Christ, commands me to do because I realize it is for the protection of myself, my family, and fellow prayer warriors.

In every confrontation, I must identify my real opponent and seek God's wisdom to know what I must do to overcome. I am learning to identify my true enemies according to the standards of God's Word.

God's Army Bible Boot Camp – Day 6

> And your feet shod with the preparation of the gospel
> of peace.
>
> —*Ephesians 6:15*

With this next piece of God's armor, I learn to protect my feet [walk] and then stand. Sometimes, a naïve and too eager soldier desiring to get into the heat of combat may often run into battle ill equipped spiritually—mentally—and emotionally—rather than standing on God's Word, and holding territory while seeking a rhema word for the situation.

Is it God's plan for believers to remain within the church boundaries promoting worldly programs to entice unbelievers into their congregations? When I am prepared spiritually to face the enemy, will God send me into enemy territory? Do my actions in His name align His Words?

I am learning the importance of following my Commander-in-Chief's orders. Jesus knows exactly what I must do in all circumstances to be victorious.

God's Army Bible Boot Camp – Day 7

> Above all, taking the shield of faith, wherewith ye shall
> be able to quench all the fiery darts of the wicked one.
>
> —*Ephesians 6:16*

The shield of faith along with prayer supersede all my armaments. "For God hath not given us the spirit of fear; but of power, and of love, and of a sound mind" *(2 Timothy 1:7)*. This verse reminds me of *James 4:7*, "Submit yourselves therefore to God. Resist the devil, and he will flee from you." "For whatsoever is born of God overcometh the world; and this is the victory that overcometh the world, even our faith. Who is he that overcometh the world, but he that believeth that Jesus is the Son of God?" *(1 John 5:4–5)*.

Faith is the imperceptible substance of things I hope for, the evidence of things I cannot see. Faith comes by hearing, and hearing by the Word [rhema] of God *(Romans 10:17)*. I trust God and remain steadfast upon His Word. The Lord's continued faithfulness builds my confidence in His ability, not my own.

It is important for me to understand the purpose of each piece of the armor of God *(Ephesians 6:10–18)*. When faced with spiritual battles—soldiers trained by God's Word with listening ears—are fully prepared to utilize their tools of engagement. I put on God's armor for my protection in the spiritual realm and in the natural.

God's Army Bible Boot Camp – Day 8

> And take the helmet of salvation, and the sword of the
> Spirit, which is the word [rhema] of God.
>
> —*Ephesians 6:17*

My knowledge of the salvation message is what protects my thoughts and keeps me mentally and emotionally ready for spiritual battle. The enemy cannot wear me down with his fiery darts of unbelief when I remain steadfast in faith. Before going into battle against my real enemy *(Ephesians 6:12),* I pray for a rhema word from the Holy Spirit.

There have been occasions in my life when I have received a rhema word while praying, yet did not see it come into being until thirty years later. Other times a rhema word produced fruit immediately. The helmet of salvation prevents the enemy from wearing me down in unbelief while I wait. Faith is the substance of things I hope to see happen in my life—the evidence of things I cannot see—so my mind is the first thing the enemy targets to undermine my faith.

As a soldier in the army of God, I must build up my faith until it is second nature. I must learn to identify my true spiritual enemies.

God's Army Bible Boot Camp – Day 9

> Praying always with all prayer and supplication in the Spirit, and watching thereunto with all perseverance and supplication for all saints; and for me, that utterance may be given unto me, that I may open my mouth boldly, to make known the mystery of the gospel, for which I am an ambassador in bonds: that therein I may speak boldly, as I ought to speak.
>
> *—Ephesians 6:18–20*

God's full armor includes earnest prayer continually in the Holy Spirit. As a soldier in the army of God, I must fearlessly speak the truth concerning the role of God's Holy Spirit in the life of a believer. The basis of what I share with others comes straight from my training manual, the Word of God.

Now that I have an overview of God's whole armor, I will train daily in His full armor. When I prepare for battle in full gear, it will become second nature to me, and I will respond instinctively when the enemy attacks.

To be a good soldier in God's army I must learn the lessons of spiritual warfare and be prepared to put them into practice.

Now is the time for me to recognize my true enemy when rapid fire assaults come against me *(Ephesians 6:12)*. The role of the church is to help one another achieve the skills we need as members in the army of God. We are to spiritually occupy His territory until Jesus returns.

Kathe S. Rumsey

God's Army Bible Boot Camp – Day 10

> But, beloved, remember ye the words [rhema] which were spoken before of the apostles of our Lord Jesus Christ; how that they told you there should be mockers in the last time who should walk after their own ungodly lusts. These be they who separate themselves, sensual, having not the Spirit. But ye, beloved, building up yourselves on your most holy faith, praying in the Holy Ghost, keep yourselves in the love of God, looking for the mercy of our Lord Jesus Christ unto eternal life. And of some have compassion, making a difference: and others save with fear, pulling them out of the fire; hating even the garment spotted by flesh.
>
> —*Jude 17–23*

The key for me to stand and not be moved by the works of the ungodly in these last days is to pray earnestly until I receive a rhema word from the Holy Spirit. Those who choose to walk in the robe of mankind's fallen nature instead of the robe of righteousness that Jesus provided, have been blinded to truth *(John 12:40; 2 Corinthians 4:1–4)*. I must not be moved by their actions. I will be victorious in all I do when I submit to my Commander-in-Chief, Jesus Christ, in everything.

God's Army Bible Boot Camp – Day 11

> I [John] indeed baptize you with water unto repentance;
> but he that cometh after me is mightier than I, whose
> shoes I am not worthy to bear: he [Jesus] shall baptize
> you with the Holy Ghost, and with fire.
>
> —*Matthew 3:11*

God provided His whole armor for me to use in spiritual battle. A vital part of His armor is praying in the Holy Spirit on all occasions *(Ephesians 6:18)*. Jesus Christ does not change; He still baptizes believers with His Holy Spirit *(Hebrews 13:8)*.

Everyone who wishes to serve in God's army must be willing to accept God's whole armor. Aa a good soldier, I cannot not pick and choose what I will put on or what equipment I will use in battle. My Commander-in-Chief, Jesus Christ, who is highly familiar with spiritual battle and battle strategies has provided a training manual, the Bible. It is crucial that I understand the basics and rely on specific instructions (rhema words) provided by the Holy Spirit as I come in contact with the evil forces of darkness of this age *(Matthew 4:4; Ephesians 6:12)*.

Many who desire to be used of God are not familiar with the role the Holy Spirit plays in a believer's life. I learned from testimonies of two ladies in my Bible study about Jesus baptizing believers with the Holy Spirit. Since one was from a Baptist background and the other a Catholic, I realized God is not limited by a denomination.

As a believer in God's Word, I must put my faith in the training manual He provided. "If ye then, being evil, know how to give good gifts unto your children; how much more shall your heavenly Father give the Holy Spirit to them that ask him? *(Luke11:13)*. "But the manifestation of the Spirit is given to every man to profit withal" *(1 Corinthians 12:7)*.

God's Army Bible Boot Camp – Day 12

It is not for you to know the times or the seasons, which the Father hath put in his own power. But ye shall receive power, after the Holy Ghost is come upon you: and ye shall be witnesses unto me both in Jerusalem, and in all Judea, and in Samaria, and unto the uttermost part of the earth.

—Acts 1:7–8

And they were all filled with the Holy Ghost, and began to speak with other tongues, as the Spirit gave them utterance.

—Acts 2:4

But this is that which was spoken by the prophet Joel; and it shall come to pass in the last days, saith God, I will pour out of my Spirit upon all flesh: and your sons and your daughters shall prophesy, your young men shall see visions, and your old men shall dream dreams; and on my servants and on my handmaidens I will pour out in those days of my Spirit; and they shall prophesy.

—Acts 2:16–18

God began pouring out His Holy Spirit on mankind on the Day of Pentecost; this was the beginning of the last days. I need the Holy Spirit in my life. As a member of the body of Christ, I ask myself often if I have witnessed God's Holy Spirit being poured out on all flesh. If God said He will do it, He will do it if we ask *(Matthew 7:11)*. The Holy Spirit is a powerful part of God's whole armor. I have not activated my daily protection without Him. I challenge myself to read as many Bible verses this week as possible that speak of God's Holy Spirit and His role in my life.

I desire to serve God according to His plan. I must continually learn from His Word how to be victorious. It is vital that I know how to listen and obey my Commander-in-Chief, Jesus Christ.

God's Army Bible Boot Camp – Day 13

I continue to challenge myself to read as many Bible verses this week that speak of God's Holy Spirit and His role in my life.

> And he set captains of war over the people, and gathered them together to him in the street of the gate of the city, and spake comfortably to them, saying, Be strong and courageous, be not afraid nor dismayed for the king of Assyria, nor for all the multitude that is with him: for there be more with us than with him: with him is an arm of flesh; but with us is the LORD our God to help us, and to fight our battles. And the people rested themselves upon the words of Hezekiah king of Judah.
>
> —*2 Chronicles 32:6–8*

Jesus said, "These things I have spoken unto you, that in me ye might have peace. In the world ye shall have tribulation: but be of good cheer [courage], I have overcome the world" *(John 16:33)*. Spiritually, there are military captains within the church. They are the ones who understand that we are not in a flesh and blood battle here on earth. These individuals have been trained by the truth of God's Word—courageously put on God's whole armor daily—and pray.

Bible Boot Camp is all about preparing my soul [mind, will, emotions] and body to withstand in this evil day. The enemy is not flesh and blood, but he is real all the same. I must build my faith in God's holy Word, which is my spiritual exercise.

As I tune my ears to hear what the Holy Spirit is saying to the churches, I will begin to recognize His leading. When given a rhema word by the Holy Spirit, I will have my marching orders. My daily armor is not complete without "praying always with all prayer and supplication in the Spirit, being watchful to this end with all perseverance and supplication for all the saints" *(Ephesians 6:18).*

God's Army Bible Boot Camp – Day 14

> And he [Jesus] said unto them, It is not for you to know the times or the seasons, which the Father hath put in his own power. But ye shall receive power, after the Holy Ghost is come upon you: and ye shall be witnesses unto me both in Jerusalem, and in all Judea, and in Samaria, and unto the uttermost part of the earth.
>
> —*Acts 1:7–8*

I do not know the times or seasons that are in God's jurisdiction alone, but God's Word makes it clear that I have a responsibility to be prepared.

Part of my preparation is to receive the power, ability, and strength to carry out the mighty works He planned for me to accomplish. The Holy Spirit has been sent so that I might have the power I need to accomplish God's plan. Praying in the Holy Spirit is a vital part of God's whole armor, and it is available to all who will ask. Since I desire to serve in God's army, I must learn the basic lessons of spiritual warfare and put on His full armor daily.

> Till we all come in the unity of the faith, and of the knowledge of the Son of God, unto a perfect man, unto the measure of the fullness of Christ: that we henceforth be no more children, tossed to and fro, and carried about with every wind of doctrine, by the sleight of men, and cunning craftiness, whereby they lie in wait to deceive; but speaking the truth in love, we are to grow up into him in all things, which is the head, even Christ; from whom the whole body fitly

joined together and compacted by that which every joint supplieth, according to the effectual working in the measure of every part, maketh increase of the body unto the edifying of itself in love.

—*Ephesians 4:13–16*

It is up to us to work as a team in the unity of faith. Scripture reminds me that no one except God the Father knows the time of Jesus' return for His church, or the exact time of the tribulation. I do not know when the battle of Armageddon will take place, except that it will follow the seven years of great tribulation. What I do know is that I am to be prepared.

God's Army Bible Boot Camp – Day 15

As a soldier in God's army, I must not have allegiance to any other god *(Exodus 20:3)*. I cannot one day say that I love God with all of my heart, and the next day participate in yoga, meditation or serve the world's idolatry. I must not be double-minded, unstable in all my ways *(James 1:8)*.

Boot camp is all about repetition. A well-trained army operates on instinct. I must prepare spiritually, mentally, and emotionally for battle. God's enemies are my enemies. My battles are not against people *(Ephesians 6:12)*. Until I can mentally accept this fact, I will never be victorious.

The enemy will continually defeat me at every turn if I fail to recognize him. God has provided His whole armor for me because He knows it is vital to my protection.

In Phase I of actual military basic training, a soldier begins to learn battle lessons. A good soldier is motivated by the realization that his or her life may depend upon it. Soldiers learn to operate as part of a troop. In God's army, I must learn the truth of His Word because the quality of my life depends upon it.

No weapon that is formed against thee shall prosper.

—*Isaiah 54:17*

God's Army Bible Boot Camp – Day 16

> Ye ask, and receive not, because ye ask amiss, that
> ye may consume it upon your lusts. Ye adulterers and
> adulteresses, know ye not that the friendship of the
> world is enmity with God? Whosoever therefore will
> be a friend of the world is the enemy of God.
>
> *—James 4:3–4*

Mentally, I prepare for spiritual warfare through the study of God's Word. His enemies are my enemies. My battles are not against other people. The quicker I accept that fact, the sooner I will know how to pray to defeat the enemy. Those who choose to make themselves an enemy of God are those who desire the things of this life, and who esteem the world systems more important than having a relationship with God.

As a prayer warrior for the kingdom of God, I recognize the influence demonic beings have on unsuspecting Christians, and people of the world. *Ephesians 6:12* identifies the four categories of spiritual beings who take their marching orders from Satan himself. In the name of Jesus, I have authority to keep the enemy on the run.

> For we wrestle not against flesh and blood, but against
> principalities, against powers, against the rulers of the
> darkness of this world, against spiritual wickedness in
> high places.
>
> *—Ephesians 6:12*

Kathe S. Rumsey

God's Army Bible Boot Camp – Day 17

> Brethren, be followers together of me [Paul], and mark
> them which walk so as ye have us for an ensample. (For
> many walk, of whom I have told you often, and now
> tell you even weeping, that they are the enemies of the
> cross of Christ: whose end is destruction, whose God
> is their belly [emotions], and whose glory is in their
> shame, who mind earthly things.) For our conversation
> is in heaven; from whence also we look for the Saviour,
> the Lord Jesus Christ; who shall change our vile body,
> that it may be fashioned like unto his glorious body,
> according to the working whereby he is able even to
> subdue all things unto himself.
>
> —*Philippians 3:17–21*

Wars and rumors of wars abound. Yet, many in the church are ill-equipped due to lack of training from the pulpit to recognize the potential enemy. Scripture says that my enemies are not other individuals. My enemies are the familiar spirits that prompt and manipulate these people.

I must train with the Word of God to identify the real enemy who influences others. For example, Satan is the father of all lies. Therefore, if others lie habitually, they operate according to the influence of Satan's kingdom, and not of God's kingdom. God is love. If I operate in unconditional love, I operate according to God's kingdom.

Mentally, and emotionally, I prepare for spiritually warfare. God's enemies are my enemies. My battles are not against flesh and blood. God provides His armor for my protection because the enemy in the unseen is vicious.

God's Army Bible Boot Camp – Day 18

> But ye, brethren, be not weary in well doing. And if any man obey not our word by this epistle, note that man, and have no company with him, that he may be ashamed. Yet count him not as an enemy, but admonish him as a brother.
>
> —*2 Thessalonians 3:13–15*

I must not grow weary or discouraged in doing what is right or considered good. My enemies will be ruthless, but not victorious as I turn to God for protection. However, God's Word says that I must stop keeping company with someone who refuses to obey Scripture. This may sound harsh but with God all things are working together for my good, and ultimately the good of others *(Romans 8:28)*. How many times have I attempted to share God's truth with someone only to have it rejected?

Occupying forces—in hostile countries—often may befriend the civilians. Soldiers have learned to build relationships even when others do not speak the same language.

It was through personal relationships I came to know Jesus Christ as my Lord and Savior. An invitation to a neighborhood craft group that evolved into a Bible study opened the door for me.

It is the individual with whom I have a personal relationship that will seek my assistance when they need help in life-threatening battles. It is my responsibility—as a good soldier of Christ—to be trained and ready at all times. God provides His whole armor because He knows it is critical for my protection.

God's Army Bible Boot Camp – Day 19

> The kingdom of heaven is likened unto a man which sowed good seed in his field: but while men slept, his enemy came and sowed tares among the wheat, and went his way. But when the blade was sprung up, and brought forth fruit, then appeared the tares also. So the servants of the householder came and said unto him, Sir, didst not thou sow good seed in thy field? From whence then hath it tares? He said unto them, An enemy hath done this. The servants said unto him, Wilt thou then that we go and gather them up? But he said Nay; lest while ye gather up the tares, ye root up also the wheat with them. Let both grow together until the harvest: and in the time of harvest I will say to the reapers, Gather ye together first the tares and bind them in bundles to burn them: but gather the wheat into my barn.
>
> *—Matthew 13:24–30*

I must remember that God's enemies will sow their tares among God's field, His church. God chooses to let the tares remain in the midst of His church for now. At the end of the age, the weeds will be gathered together and burnt. The wheat will be brought together into His barn.

As a soldier, I am being trained to take my marching orders from my Commander-in-Chief, Jesus Christ. I am not to operate according to what I see or my emotions. I put on the whole armor of God daily.

God's Army Bible Boot Camp – Day 20

Am I prepared to Serve God? I must test myself.

> Thou therefore endure hardness, as a good soldier of
> Jesus Christ. No man that warreth entangleth himself
> with the affairs of this life; that he may please him who
> hath chosen him to be a soldier.
>
> *—2 Timothy 2:3–4.*

Spiritually, mentally, and emotionally, I prepare for war. My battle maneuvers are not against flesh and blood. Circumstances appear believable, I must not fall prey to Satan's schemes while blaming others. The devil will attempt to make me consider family members or friends as my enemy, yet it is not people who are my real enemies *(Ephesians 6:12).* Until I grasp this truth from God's Word, I endanger my relationships, giving Satan a foothold. He knows a house, or a nation divided will fall. This is his plan. He does not wish for God's children to be victorious. He is looking for whom he may destroy.

As a soldier in God's army I know from my training manual— the Bible—how the enemy strategizes and how he tries to trip me up. I must not be fooled. The enemy uses the same combat plan over and over; he plays off my weaknesses. In the name of Jesus Christ, I have the authority to counterattack the enemy's plans before he can dominate me. As a prayer warrior, I am being trained offensively as well as the defensively.

God's Army Bible Boot Camp – Day 21

> This charge I [Paul] commit unto thee, son Timothy,
> according to the prophecies in which went before
> on thee, that thou by them you mightiest war a good
> warfare; holding faith, and a good conscience; which
> some having put away concerning faith have made
> shipwreck; of whom is Hymenaeus and Alexander;
> whom I have delivered unto Satan, that may learn not
> to blaspheme.
>
> —*1 Timothy 1:18–20*

Bible Boot Camp is all about preparing me spiritually, mentally, and emotionally before I find myself in battle with the enemy. It is the Word of God—that I diligently practice daily—that keeps me combat ready. My enemies are not other people. My enemies are the demonic forces of Satan's camp. They attempt to rob what legally belongs to me as a joint heir with Christ Jesus.

Before I was a born-again believer, I had placed my faith in my abilities or my denomination rather than the Word of God. Many church members today are losing the battle against God's enemies because they have not learned the importance of the Holy Spirit and God's whole armor in their life.

Jesus explicated his followers not to go out into the world until they received "power from on high" *(Luke 24:49)*. In my life, the Holy Spirit makes the difference as to whether I walk in victory or defeat. Currently, many in the church compromise with the unsaved world where Satan rules. Without the armor of God, their lives are being devoured.

God's Army Bible Boot Camp – Day 22

> For though we walk in the flesh, we do not war after the flesh; (For the weapons of our warfare are not carnal, but mighty through God to the pulling of strong holds.) casting down imaginations, and every high thing that exalteth itself against the knowledge of God, and bringing into captivity every thought to the obedience of Christ; and having a readiness to revenge all disobedience, when your obedience is fulfilled.
>
> *—2 Corinthians 10:3–6*

I am learning that those enlisted in the army of God conduct their lives differently than other individuals. God's armor is not of this world; it has the power to make all things possible. Jesus provides me with His name and the authority I need to obtain victory here on earth. If I choose not to listen to what the Holy Spirit is saying to the churches, I cannot prepare for battle. Satan is looking for whom he may devour *(1 Peter 5:8).*

I must diligently prepare my mind for spiritual warfare. My battles are not against flesh and blood *(Ephesians 6:12).* Bible Boot Camp may seem repetitive at times, yet the truths of God's Word will set me free and enable me to become a victorious overcomer.

Kathe S. Rumsey

God's Army Bible Boot Camp – Day 23

When challenged by a spiritual enemy that attempts to lay physical symptoms of ill-health on my body, I have learned to rely on what the Holy Spirit has taught me over a span of thirty-plus years.

Normally, I would call the mature believers of the church first and ask for prayer *(James 5:14)*. However, because I am walking through Bible Boot Camp training, I challenged myself to see what I would do if I did not have mature, biblically trained members of God's army available to pray for me.

On occasion, soldiers may find themselves in situations without backup. It is times like these that I must draw on what I know; I must seek God for wisdom in these situations, then stand firm. Throughout the day, I pray in my prayer language when not sure how to pray *(Romans 8:26)*.

While sorting through notes from past years—times when my prayer partner and I had prayed for others facing serious health conditions—I realized most were life and death situations. The first thing I noticed with all of these prayer requests happened within a three-year span from the time we were born-again; we were still new believers. We had childlike faith; we believed everything the Word of God said, and we had attentive ears to hear the Holy Spirit.

The enemy tempts us to name our physical symptoms and take ownership of them. The Holy Spirit brought to my mind *Psalm 107:2*, "Let the redeemed of the LORD say so, whom he hath redeemed from the hand of the enemy." I began to watch what I was speaking concerning my symptoms—and the morning that followed—I awoke almost completely symptom free. I then put *James 4:7* into action, "Submit yourselves therefore to God.

Resist the devil, and he will flee from you." God made a way of escape for me. I overcame the temptation to name and talk about my symptoms. Satan looks for whom He may devour. I prepare for battle spiritually, mentally, and emotionally with the help of the Holy Spirit. My battles are not against flesh and blood.

Kathe S. Rumsey

God's Army Bible Boot Camp – Day 24

> Then was Jesus led up of the spirit into the wilderness
> to be tempted by the devil.
>
> *—Matthew 4:1*

> And when the tempter came to him [Jesus], he said,
> If thou be the Son of God, command that these
> stones be made bread. But he answered and said,
> It is written, Man shall not live by bread alone, but
> by every word [rhema] that proceedeth out of the
> mouth of God.
>
> *—Matthew 4:3–4.*

> And when the devil had ended all the temptation, he
> departed from him [Jesus] for a season.
>
> *—Luke 4:13*

Just as the Spirit led Jesus into a forsaken desolate place where the
enemy tempted Him, I too will face temptations. Jesus said that I
am to be courageous because He had overcome the world *(John
16:33)*. I overcome by His blood and the words of my testimony
(Revelation 12:11). The things I overcome strengthen my faith.

As a soldier of Christ, I live my life by the rhema words
revealed to me by the Holy Spirit. These words may come from a
verse that comes to life as I read God's written word. It may also
be something the Holy Spirit reveals to my spirit for a particular
situation. A rhema word may be a word that comes to me as I
pray about my circumstances, or those of others. I train my ears
to hear my marching orders in all situations based upon what I
learn from my training manual, the Bible. An army does not run

out into the battlefield without a strategic plan. It is the same with God's army. I must take my marching orders from God, having ears to hear what the Holy Spirit reveals to me.

Believers who enlist in the army of God conduct their lives differently than the rest of humankind. God's armor is not of this world. I have the authority in Jesus' name to be victorious here on earth. I must choose to be obedient to my Commander-in-Chief's marching orders. Satan is looking for whom He may devour. I choose for it not to be me, nor those I love.

Kathe S. Rumsey

God's Army Bible Boot Camp – Day 25

Thou therefore endure hardness as a good soldier of Jesus Christ. No man that warreth entangleth himself with the affairs of this life; that he may please him who hath chosen him to be a soldier.

—2 Timothy 2:3–4

Then Jesus said unto the chief priests, and captains of the temple, and the elders, which were come to him, Be ye come out, as against a thief, with swords and staves? When I was daily with you in the temple, ye stretched forth no hands against me; but this is your hour, and the power of darkness.

—Luke 22:52–53

Jesus did not respond to the community and religious leaders as the world would respond. He recognized that He was dealing with the ruling spiritual forces of the hour. Jesus knew that for His life to be a redemptive sacrifice, God alone allowed the power of darkness control for that particular season *(John 7:30; 19:11)*. "For the mystery of iniquity doth already work: only he who now letteth will let, until he be taken out of the way" *(2 Thessalonians 2:7)*.

Daily, we experience the pressures and concerns of this life. Jesus has enlisted me to serve in His army. There is coming a time when the power of darkness will have full reign and authority to govern. In the meantime, the good soldiers of Christ serve as an occupying force. I must take my marching orders from Jesus Christ—the Word of God—through the Holy Spirit.

Christians who enlist in the army of God conduct their lives differently than the rest of humankind. God's armor is not of this world but provides my protection from His enemies. I have the power and authority in the name of Jesus Christ to obtain victory here on earth. If I choose not to listen to what the Holy Spirit is saying to the churches, I cannot prepare for spiritual combat. Satan is looking for whom He may devour. My battles are not against flesh and blood. A well-trained soldier in the army of God knows his authority in Christ Jesus and uses it.

Kathe S. Rumsey

God's Army Bible Boot Camp – Day 26

> Judas then, having received a band of men and officers
> from the chief priests and Pharisees, cometh thither
> with lanterns and torches and weapons.
>
> —*John 18:3*

> Then said Jesus unto Peter, Put thy sword into the
> sheath: the cup which my Father hath given me,
> shall I not drink it?
>
> —*John 18:11*

According to *John 18:3*, Judas brought a company of 600 fighting men to arrest Jesus. This shows the lengths the spiritual forces of the devil will go to in order to stop God's messengers of truth. Jesus was well aware of all the things that would come upon Him, yet went forward and said to those who had come to arrest Him, "Whom seek ye?" *(John 18:4)*.

I would have been intimidated, but Jesus knew His hour had come. Jesus had already prayed and prepared for His Father's will to be accomplished *(John 3:16)*. Jesus is my example of being well prepared for anything that the enemy might bring against me. I choose to do my heavenly Father's will. Jesus received His commission from His Father; He prayed not only for Himself, but also for his disciples as He faced His vicious opposition. Jesus remained laser-focused on what He had to do; He did not allow the 600 fighting men or His human emotions to sidetrack His assignment.

However, Peter—who neither watched nor prayed, but slept while Jesus prayed—was not prepared for what was coming *(Matthew 26:40–46)*.

As a soldier of Christ, I serve as an occupying force. I take my marching orders from Jesus Christ through the Holy Spirit. The church Jesus is building must have ears to hear the Holy Spirit.

God's people have the authority in Jesus' name to obtain victory here on earth. Satan is looking for whom He may devour. I choose for it not to be me.

God's Army Bible Boot Camp – Day 27

And I saw the beast, and the kings of the earth, and their armies, gathered together to make war against him [Jesus] that sat on the horse, and against his army. And the beast was taken, and with him the false prophet that wrought miracles before him, with which he deceived them that had received the mark of the beast, and them that worshiped his image. These both were cast alive into the lake of fire burning with brimstone.

—Revelation 19:19–20

And I saw three unclean spirits like frogs come out of the mouth of the dragon [Satan], and out of the mouth of the beast, and out of the mouth of the false prophet. For they are spirits of devils, working miracles, which go forth unto the kings of the earth and of the whole world, to gather them to the battle of that great day of God Almighty. Behold, I [Jesus] come as a thief. Blessed is he that watcheth, and keepeth his garments, lest he walk naked, and they see his shame.

—Revelation 16:13–15.

Scripture says that just as Christ is head of the church, the husband is head of the wife. Satan deceived the woman first; then, Adam failed to obey God, and listened to Eve *(Genesis 3:1–7)*.

The New Testament uses the word *frogs* only one time. These refer to "spirits of devils." I went to the Old Testament to read the verses that mentioned frogs. It was helpful to understand what spews out of the mouths of Satan and his followers. I must never forget other individuals are not my enemies. The powers of darkness that influence people to do Satan's bidding are my enemy.

There is coming a time when Satan and his hierarchy will no longer be in control or have the freedom to govern. In the meantime, as a good soldier of Christ, I serve as a member of His occupying force. I take my marching orders from Jesus Christ through the inspiration of the Holy Spirit.

Kathe S. Rumsey

God's Army Bible Boot Camp – Day 28

> But he [Jesus], knowing their thoughts, said unto them, Every kingdom divided against itself is brought to desolation; and a house divided against a house falleth. If Satan also be divided against himself, how shall his kingdom stand? because ye say that I cast out devils through Beelzebub. And if I with the finger of God cast out devils, no doubt the kingdom of God is come upon you. When a strong man armed keepeth his palace, his goods are in peace.
>
> —*Luke 11:17–18, 20–21*

When Christians allowed the removal of God from every aspect of our lives, my nation became divided. America is no longer at peace. According to Scripture, a divided kingdom will fall. This is what the enemy looks for in a victim. He sows division among believers, households, and nations.

My country will not survive if I allow division to persist. I must pray. Daily, I must put on the whole armor of God. I have the power and authority in the name of Jesus Christ to obtain victory here on earth. Bible Boot Camp is preparing me to identify God's enemies and to instinctively respond to their attacks according to my training manual, the Bible.

God's Army Bible Boot Camp – Day 29

> But when a stronger than he shall come upon him,
> and overcome him, he taketh from him all his armour
> wherein he trusted, and divideth his spoils. He that
> is not with me [Jesus] is against me; And he that
> gathereth not with me scattereth.
>
> —*Luke 11:22–23*

This verse reminds me of a Christian who may sit in church every Sunday and listen to a pastor's sermon based upon unsound doctrine, or the current trends of the world. Because these believers attend a recognized denomination—with a pastor vetted and hired by a church board—they believe everything preached without questioning what they hear.

I have learned that I must spend time in prayer with the Holy Spirit of truth and God's Word to verify what I hear. It is critical for me to study the Bible for myself and with others. I personally desire to know what God's Word truly means, and I utilize every tool I have at my disposal. However, since I cannot know everything—and I desire to be accountable to God—I must not forsake gathering with other believers.

Unlike the world, I must continually look for truth and be open to learning. I believe God's Word in its entirety. I do not want to be led astray by false teaching contrary to Jesus' doctrine. Christians—who choose not to listen to what the Holy Spirit is saying to the churches—will be unprepared when the enemy attacks. Satan is looking for whom He may devour. I choose to be trained and prepared. I choose not to be one of Satan's victims. The moment the enemy comes against some believers—their trust in God falters—leaving them doubtful and defeated.

God's Army Bible Boot Camp – Day 30

> And even things without life giving sound, whether
> pipe or harp, except they give a distinction in the
> sounds, how shall it be known what is piped or
> harped? For if the trumpet give an uncertain sound,
> who shall prepare himself for battle? So likewise
> ye, except ye utter by the tongue words easy to be
> understood, how shall it be known what is spoken?
> for ye shall speak into the air. There are, it may be, so
> many kinds of voices in the world, and none of them
> is without signification. Therefore if I know not the
> meaning of the voice, I shall be unto him that speaketh
> a barbarian, and he that speaketh shall be a barbarian
> unto me. Even so ye, forasmuch as ye are zealous of
> spiritual gifts, seek that ye may excel to the edifying
> of the church. Wherefore let him that speaketh in an
> unknown tongue pray that he may interpret.
>
> —*1 Corinthians 14:7–13*

As a soldier heading into battle, I must have a means of communication with upper command; I need to have up-to-date information. The determining factor in any victory is to possess the data concerning the enemy's maneuvers.

Jesus said, "I have yet many things to say unto you, but ye cannot bear them now. Howbeit when he, the Spirit of truth, is come, he will guide you into all truth: for he shall not speak of himself; but whatsoever he shall hear, that shall he speak: and he will shew you things to come" *(John 16:12–13)*. When the Holy Spirit speaks, I must have ears to hear Him *(Revelation 3:13)*.

God's Army Bible Boot Camp – Day 31

> For thus says the LORD; after 70 years are complete at Babylon I will visit you and perform My good word [desirable duty required] toward you, and cause you to return to this place. For I know the thoughts that I think toward you, says the LORD, thoughts of peace and not evil, to give you a future and a hope. Then you will call upon Me and go and pray to Me, and I will listen to you, And you will seek Me and find Me, when you search for Me with all your heart. I will be found by you, says the LORD, and I will bring you back from your captivity; I will gather you from all nations and from all the places where I have driven you to the place which I caused you to be carried away captive. Because you have said, The LORD has raised up prophets for us in Babylon.
>
> —*Jeremiah 29:10–15*

These were the words of Jeremiah the prophet sent from Jerusalem to the remainder of the elders who were carried away captive. While reading this, I saw a parallel between the *baby boom* generation and Israel. The first of the boomers were born in 1946 and Israel became a nation in 1948. Contrary to what we may think, this generation has been wandering in the wilderness. God has a plan for us, and it is not what we see happening in America today. His plan is for peace, and not evil; it is to give us and others a future and a hope. We—as a generation—allowed the spirit of rebellion to take our nation. We are reaping the consequences of our sinful choices.

As a whole, the *baby boomers* were the last generation in America trained in the truth of God's Word. Only God can heal our land. My marching orders come from *2 Chronicles 7:14*. I must take my stand through repentance and prayer.

God's armor is not of this world. I have the power and authority in the name of Jesus Christ to obtain victory here on earth. If I choose not to listen to what the Holy Spirit is saying to the churches in the Book of Revelation, I will be unprepared for battle. Satan is looking for whom he may devour. My battles are not against flesh and blood. Until I completely understand this principle and put it into practice, I will never experience victory; I will suffer defeat.

God's Army Bible Boot Camp – Day 32

> Pray for the peace of Jerusalem; they shall prosper that love thee. Peace be within thy walls, and prosperity within thy palaces. For my brethren and companions' sakes, I will now say, Peace be within you. Because of the house of the LORD our God I will seek thy good.
>
> *—Psalm 122:6–9*

While America remained a loyal friend to Israel, she prospered. We cannot turn our backs on Israel and expect God to bless America. I must ask God intently—beg Him if you will—to bring peace to Jerusalem. Evil forces of darkness in the spiritual realm attempt to control what takes place in Jerusalem.

The marching orders for America's church come from *2 Chronicles 7:14.* Only God can heal our land.

As an enlisted soldier in the army of God, I must conduct my life differently from those of the world. I must repent and take my stand in prayer. God's armor is not of this world. I have authority in the name of Jesus to obtain victory here on earth. I must pray and listen to the Holy Spirit for a rhema word if I desire to be fully armed for spiritual battle. Satan is looking for whom He may devour. I choose not to be unprepared. I choose not to be his victim.

God's Army Bible Boot Camp – Day 33

Then the high priest rose up, and all they that were with him, (which is the sect of the Sadducees,) and were filled with indignation, and laid their hands on the apostles, and put them in the common prison. But the angel of the Lord by night opened the prison doors, and brought them forth, and said, Go, stand and speak in the temple to the people all the words [rhema] of this life. And when they heard that they entered into the temple early in the morning, and taught. But the high priest came, and they that were with him, and called the council together, and all the senate of the children of Israel, and sent to the prison to have them brought. Saying, The prison truly we found shut with all safety, and the keepers standing without before the doors: but when we had opened, we found no man within. Then came one and told them, saying, Behold, the men whom ye put in prison are standing in the temple, and teaching the people.

—Acts 5:17–21, 23, 25.

Nothing can hold me in prison when I am willing to be obedient. It does not matter what things appear to be; it only matters that I am willing to follow the commands of my Commander-in-Chief—Jesus Christ—when He gives me my orders. With God, absolutely nothing is impossible!

God's Army Bible Boot Camp – Day 34

> The wise heart will receive commandments: but a prating fool shall fall. It is as sport to a fool to do mischief: but a man of understanding hath wisdom.
>
> *—Proverbs 10:8, 23*

The wise soldier in God's army reverences the Lord. Their actions demonstrate their moral character. My battles are not with other people *(Ephesians 6:12).*

If I patiently listen for God's words—have ears to hear the Holy Spirit—I will receive His commands for action. From Proverbs, I learned that a warrior of understanding with insight, ability, and discretion is one of a kind. He is not like every other soldier in the ranks. There is something different. This soldier does not verbally reveal their every thought. He does not provide the enemy with the commands he has received from his Commander-in-Chief, Jesus Christ.

I must choose my words wisely and only speak God's plans in a *need-to-know* situation. Only a foolish soldier goes about spouting the plans that are going to be put into action. I am learning to be a wise soldier in God's army and to be discrete when He reveals His plan with me. During wartime, soldiers are not authorized to inform their loved ones where their assignment is taking them, and for good reason.

Kathe S. Rumsey

God's Army Bible Boot Camp – Day 35

And Jesus answering saith unto them, Have faith in God. For verily I say unto you, That whosoever shall say unto this mountain, Be thou removed, and be thou cast into the sea; and shall not doubt in his heart, but shall believe that those things which he saith shall come to pass; he shall have whatsoever he saith. Therefore I [Jesus] say unto you, What things soever ye desire, when ye pray, believe that ye receive them, and ye shall have them.

—Mark 11:22–24

When I read in *Luke 8:26–39* that Jesus cast a legion of demons out of a man, permitting them to enter the swine, it became clear that people are not my enemies; demonic forces influence people and their actions. As a soldier of God, I must not be intimidated. I am to be of good cheer (courage) because Jesus has overcome the world. Prayer moves mountains.

With all the demonic activity taking place around the world, there is a possibility that I may encounter a spirit of intimidation. I must continue to prepare to stand up to the spiritual bullies I meet. God did not give me a spirit of fear. He gave me a sound mind. Just as David faced a giant with a sling shot and five stones and came out victorious, I may face similar bullies and I need to be prepared.

God's Army Bible Boot Camp – Day 36

> Then Peter opened his mouth, and said, Of a truth
> I perceive that God is no respecter of persons: but
> in every nation he that feareth him, and worketh
> righteousness, is accepted with him. The word which
> God sent unto the children of Israel, preaching peace
> by Jesus Christ: (he is Lord of all:) That word [rhema],
> I say, ye know, which was published; throughout all
> Judea, and began from Galilee, after the baptism which
> John preached; How God anointed Jesus of Nazareth
> with the Holy Ghost and with power: who went about
> doing good, and healing all that were oppressed of the
> devil; for God was with him.
>
> *—Acts 10: 34–38*

Jesus promised that the Father would send the Holy Spirit in His name and that we would do greater things than He did *(John 14:12, 26)*. Each member of the body of Christ has been assigned a specific task. The church has been given the power of God to accomplish the work. Yet—how many who are oppressed by Satan or demon spirits—have been made whole?

Which kingdom is superior: the kingdom of God or the kingdom of the devil? As a soldier in God's army, I do not advance without orders—a rhema word—from my Commander-in-Chief, Jesus Christ, through the Holy Spirit. I take my orders from no other.

God's Army Bible Boot Camp – Day 37

Nehemiah confesses to God.

> We have dealt very corruptly against thee, and have not kept the commandments, nor the statutes, nor the judgments, which thou commandedst thy servant Moses. Remember, I beseech thee, the word that thou commandedst thy servant Moses, saying, If ye transgress, I will scatter you abroad among the nations: but if ye turn unto me, and keep my commandments, and do them; though there were of you cast out unto the uttermost part of the heaven, yet will I gather them from thence, and will bring them unto the place that I have chosen to set my name there.
>
> *—Nehemiah 1:7–9*

America wandered from her godly foundation because God's army has not stood its guard and spiritually occupy her land. Christians allowed God's Word and prayer to be removed from schools *(Proverbs 22:6)*. The sleeping church has allowed God's Commandments to be removed from every public arena *(Exodus 20:1–17)*. Through prayer, in the name of Jesus Christ, the army of God has the authority to reinstate these valuable mandates of righteousness from God.

As a soldier in God's occupying force, I conduct my life differently than that of this world. God's armor is spiritual. Only God makes all things possible. I have the authority in the name of Jesus Christ to obtain victory here on earth. I choose to listen to the Holy Spirit. I cannot prepare for spiritual battle without Him. Satan is looking for whom He may devour. The skirmishes the devil wages against me are not flesh and blood battles, even though they come through the actions of others.

God's Army Bible Boot Camp – Day 38

SAVE me, O God; for the waters are come in unto my soul. I sink in deep mire, where there is no standing: I am come into deep waters, where the floods overflow me. I am weary of my crying: my throat is dried: my eyes fail while I wait for my God. They that hate me without a cause are more than the hairs of mine head: they that would destroy me, being my enemies wrongfully, then I restored that which I took not away.

—Psalms 69:1–4

David was a mighty warrior yet he experienced times when he felt his enemies were more than he could resist. Through his testimony I have learned—that in spite of David's seemingly impossible situations—he waited for and depended upon God alone to rescue him from his enemies.

We all have experienced times of feeling overwhelmed by the cares of this life and our trials of faith. Situations arise that I did not cause, yet I must restore peace. Without God however, I will be unable to do anything. Just as David cried out to God, I must cry out for God's wisdom. Only then, will I be a victorious soldier.

Kathe S. Rumsey

God's Army Bible Boot Camp – Day 39

> Thus says the LORD of hosts, the God of Israel,
> unto all that are carried away captives, whom I have
> caused to be carried away from Jerusalem unto
> Babylon; build ye houses, and dwell in them; and
> plant gardens, and eat the fruit of them; And seek
> the peace of the city whither I have caused you to
> be carried away captives, and pray unto the LORD
> for it: for in the peace thereof shall ye have peace.
>
> —*Jeremiah 29:4–5, 7*

As a good soldier of God, I must remember I have a personal covenant relationship with Him. The Father, Son, and Holy Spirit each have a role in my development as a prayer warrior. There are times when I will go through harsh training to prepare me for the next battle. God allows difficulties in my life not to punish me or to break me, but quite the contrary; He builds and strengthens me so the enemy no longer has the spiritual advantage over me.

I live in a nation once greatly influenced by God and His Word. Those who came before me willingly sacrificed all for the good of their faith, their family, their community, and their new nation. Sadly, we have become a nation greatly influenced by the gods of Babylon. However, it is never too late to return to Yahweh.

God's army operates in the authority and training He provides to rebuild our nation. I must not misuse the time I have for prayer. I must redeem the time because the days are evil *(Ephesians 5:16).*

God's Army Bible Boot Camp – Day 40

> Whoso rewardeth evil for good, evil shall not depart from his house. The beginning of strife is as when one letteth out water: therefore leave off contention, before it be meddled with. He that justifieth the wicked, and he that condemneth the just, even they are an abomination to the LORD.
>
> —*Proverbs 17:13–15*

Prayer warriors in God's army stand in the gap between good and evil. Jesus' church is to occupy until He returns. I see evil rewarded by the lack of consequences for wrongdoing, and no one stops the evil behavior. Proverbs says strife is as releasing water. Once it starts, strife spreads everywhere and is difficult to contain. Yet God judges both—those who *allow* evil and those who *vindicate* evil—to be an abomination to Him.

As a soldier in God's occupying forces, I must pray and take a stand for His kingdom without wavering. This is not the hour for me to be lukewarm in my faith. When things seem to be overwhelming, I must stop and take a breath. Rejoice! God asks me to take only one day at a time.

God's Army Bible Boot Camp – Day 41

> But love ye your enemies, and do good, and lend,
> hoping for nothing again; and your reward shall be
> great, and ye shall be the children of the Highest: for
> he is kind unto the unthankful and to the evil. Be ye
> therefore merciful, as your Father also is merciful.
> Judge not, and ye shall not be judged: condemn not,
> and ye shall not be condemned: forgive, and ye shall
> be forgiven.
>
> —*Luke 6:35–37*

This was the most difficult verse for me to obey when I was first born-again. The Holy Spirit led me to *Ephesians 6:12*. "For we wrestle not against flesh and blood, but against principalities, against powers, against the rulers of the darkness of this world, against spiritual wickedness in high places." When I perceived my enemies to be people, I failed to recognize the real enemy that influences these individuals.

Luke 6:35–37 reminds me to love those that are indifferent toward me just as God loved me when I was indifferent toward Him. How can we call ourselves children of God and not obey His Word? I must follow the example of my Commander-in-Chief, Jesus Christ. Scripture exhorts me to judge not, condemn not, forgive and I will be forgiven. If I choose not to forgive others, how can I be forgiven? Forgiveness is a free will choice I must make. How do I expect to be victorious if I refuse to follow orders from my Commander?

God's Army Bible Boot Camp – Day 42

NOW the word of the LORD came unto Jonah the
son of Amittai, saying, Arise, go Nineveh, that great
city, and cry against it; for their wickedness is come
up before me. But Jonah arose to flee unto Tarshish
from the presence of the LORD, and went down to
Joppa; and he found a ship going to Tarshish: so he
paid the fare thereof, and went down into it, to go
with them unto Tarshish from the presence of the
LORD. But the LORD sent out a great wind into the
sea, and there was a mighty tempest in the sea, so
that the ship was like to be broken.

Then the mariners were afraid, and cried every
man unto his god, and cast forth the wares that were
in the ship into the sea, to lighten it of them. But
Jonah was gone down into the sides of the ship; and
he lay, and was fast asleep. So the shipmaster came
to him, and said unto him, What meanest thou, O
sleeper? arise, call upon thy God, if so be that God
will think upon us, that we perish not. So they took
up Jonah, and cast him forth into the sea: and the
sea ceased from her raging. Then the men feared the
LORD exceedingly, and offered a sacrifice unto the
LORD, and made vows. Now the LORD had prepared
a great fish to swallow up Jonah. And Jonah was in
the belly of the fish three days and three nights.

—Jonah 1:1–6, 15–17

God had a contingency plan in case Jonah failed to obey. God
knew Jonah would not obey so He provided the storm and the

fish to bring about His plan. What is He asking of me? What is He asking of His prayer warriors?

Sometime ago, I read where Tim Tebow saw a man having a seizure; he leaned over the edge of the stadium barrier, reached down where the man was laying, and laid hands on the man and prayed. It is difficult to imagine doing something like that in a public place where many of the media cannot wait to make fun of our faith. God used Tim's faith and actions to demonstrate courage.

Until I am willing to do whatever it takes to obey God, I am not ready to serve God and Him alone. I must prepare spiritually, mentally, and emotionally to be ready to serve in God's army.

God's Army Bible Boot Camp – Day 43

When an enlisted man or woman enters the military, they do not provide their own clothing, food, shelter, or weapons. When believers enter the army of God, they do not provide their own spiritual armor, food, shelter, and weapons. God is our provider. His Word is our training manual. Everything we need to overcome is found on the pages of the Bible.

> If ye then be not able to do that thing which is least, why take ye thought for the rest? But rather seek ye the kingdom of God; and all these things shall be added unto you.
>
> —*Luke 12:26, 31*

As a volunteer recruit in the army of God I conduct my life differently than those of the world. God provides His full armor for my protection in the battles I face. I have the power and authority in the name of Jesus Christ to obtain victory here on earth. I choose to hear what the Holy Spirit is saying to me. Without the direction and guidance of the Holy Spirit, I cannot adequately prepare for spiritual battle. Satan is looking for whom he may devour. I choose not to be his victim.

God's Army Bible Boot Camp – Day 44

> But God composed the body, having given greater
> honor to that part which lacks it, that there should be
> no schism in the body, but that the members should
> have the same care for one another. And if one member
> suffers, all the members suffer with it; or if one member
> is honored, all the members rejoice with it. Now you
> are the body of Christ, and members individually. And
> God has appointed these in the church: first apostles,
> second prophets, third teachers, after that miracles,
> then gifts of healing, helps, administration, varieties
> of tongues.
>
> —*1 Corinthians 12:24–28 (NKJV)*

Individual soldiers in God's army have God-given abilities. My Commander-in-Chief—Jesus Christ with the Holy Spirit—assigns my position within the body of Christ. The Holy Spirit gives to some the free gift of healing for the body of Christ. He gives to some the ability to aid others in need. He gives to some the ability to lead. He gives to some the varieties of tongues. Not one of these roles is of greater honor than another. The role God created me to fulfill is the perfect one for me.

The person God chooses to be a pastor is no greater than the individual that cleans the church. In the army of God, the invalid who remains in bed praying for the needs of the church is equally as valuable in God's kingdom as the one He sends into the mission field.

God created each one of us for a specific purpose. He appointed each role in the church to carry out a specific assignment. I know my assignment and prepare for it daily. The body of Christ needs each member operating in their designated position, otherwise the body malfunctions. Time is of the essence *(Ephesians 5:16)*. I must wake up and fall in line—outfitted in God's full armor—and train for spiritual battle.

God's Army Bible Boot Camp – Day 45

> BE merciful unto me, O God: for man would swallow
> me up; he fighting daily oppresseth me. Mine enemies
> would daily swallow me up: for they be many that
> fight against me, O thou most High. What time I am
> afraid, I will trust in thee. In God I will praise his
> word, in God I have put my trust; I will not fear what
> flesh can do unto me. Every day they wrest my words;
> all their thoughts are against me for evil.
>
> —*Psalms 56:1–5*

The key is to trust in God and His plan. God has not given me
a spirit of fear. Jesus told me in His Word, "Be of good cheer
[courage]" because He has already overcome the world. I
overcome by His blood and the word of my testimony *(Revelation
12:11)*. Jesus won all my victories at Calvary. Until I understand
who my enemy truly is, I will fail to recognize the victory Jesus
provides for me *(Ephesians 6:12)*.

I make a choice daily to either serve God or to fall prey to the
tricks of the devil. Soldiers are trained to make the correct split-
second choices when faced by their enemies. The more familiar I
am with the Word of God, the quicker I can make the best choice
when under the fire of the enemy.

God's Army Bible Boot Camp – Day 46

> IF it had not been the LORD who was on our side, now may Israel say; If it had not been the LORD who was on our side, when men rose up against us: then they had swallowed us up quick, when their wrath was kindled against us: then the waters had overwhelmed us, the stream had gone over our soul: then the proud waters had gone over our soul. Blessed be the LORD, who hath not given us as a prey to their teeth. Our soul is escaped as a bird out of the snare of the fowlers: the snare is broken, and we are escaped. Our help is in the name of the LORD, who made heaven and earth.
>
> *—Psalm 124:1–8*

No matter what I see before me, my help is in the name of the LORD who made heaven and earth. Nothing man can do to me can defeat me because my God is greater. I can be courageous because Jesus overcame the world. As a soldier in God's army, I place my confidence in my Commander-in-Chief, Jesus Christ, to provide wisdom and direction. God offers His full armor and His Word for my protection *(Ephesians 6:10–18)*.

God's Army Bible Boot Camp – Day 47

> For whatsoever is born of God overcometh the world:
> and this is the victory that overcometh the world, even
> our faith. Who is he who overcometh the world, but
> he that believeth that Jesus is the Son of God? He
> that believeth on the Son of God hath the witness in
> himself; he that believeth not God hath made him a
> liar; because he believeth not the record that God gave
> of his Son. And this is the confidence that we have in
> him, that, if we ask any thing according to his will, he
> heareth us: and if we know that he hear us, whatsoever
> we ask, we know that we have the petitions that we
> desire of him.
>
> *—1 John 5:4–5, 10, 14–15*

God's soldiers are able to conquer the world system because of our confident belief in God and His Word. I do not hope God is real—I am confident He is who He says He is—and He is not limited by man's limitations. When I pray and obey, I operate in the same authority Jesus walked in while on earth. Jesus overcame the world. God promises me that I can overcome by Jesus' blood and the word of my testimony.

God's armor and weapons are not of this world. I have the power and authority in the name of Jesus to obtain victory here on earth. Satan is looking for whom he may devour. I must prepare spiritually, mentally, and emotionally for the battles I face. Scripture says my battles are not against flesh and blood *(Ephesians 6:12).*

God's Army Bible Boot Camp – Day 48

Am I prepared to serve God? I must test myself.

> I have pursued mine enemies, and overtaken them:
> neither did I turn again till they were consumed. I
> have wounded them that they were not able to rise:
> they are fallen under my feet. For thou hast girded
> me with strength unto the battle: thou hast subdued
> under me those that rose up against me. Thou hast
> delivered me from the strivings of the people; and
> thou hast made me the head of the heathen: a people
> whom I have not known shall serve me. As soon as
> they hear of me, they shall obey me; the strangers
> shall submit to me. The strangers shall fade away,
> and be afraid out of their close places. The LORD
> liveth; and blessed be my rock; and let the God of
> my salvation be exalted. It is God that avengeth me,
> and subdueth the people under me. He delivereth me
> from mine enemies: yea, thou liftest me up above
> those that rise up against me: thou hast delivered me
> from the violent man. Therefore will I give thanks
> unto thee, O LORD, among the heathen, and sing
> praises unto thy name. Great deliverance giveth he
> to his king; and sheweth mercy to his anointed, to
> David, and to his seed for evermore.
>
> —*Psalm 18:37–39, 43–50*

God has a plan and a purpose for my life. My training has
taught me that the battles I face are not against flesh and blood.
God is my protector. He delivers His own from violent men. I must

put on the whole armor of God and stand strong *(Ephesians 6:10–18)*. Jesus has promised never to forsake me nor leave me even to the ends of this age. I will rejoice because I am not alone. As a prayer warrior, I will seek God's wisdom in all circumstances. I will pray for a rhema word to stand upon when confronted by an enemy.

God's Army Bible Boot Camp – Day 49

> Beloved, when I gave all diligence to write unto you of the common salvation, it was needful for me to write unto you, and exhort you that ye should earnestly contend for the faith which was once delivered unto the saints. For there are certain men crept in unawares, who were before of old ordained to this condemnation, ungodly men, turning the grace of our God into lasciviousness, and denying the only Lord God, and our Lord Jesus Christ. I will therefore put you in remembrance though ye once knew this, how that the Lord, having saved the people out of the land of Egypt, afterward destroyed them that believed not.
>
> *—Jude vs. 3–5*

Jesus said,

> I know thy works, and thy labour, thy patience, and how thou canst not bear them which are evil: and thou hast tried them which say they are apostles [messengers], and are not, and hast found them liars: and hast borne, and hast patience, and for my name's sake hast not fainted. Nevertheless I have somewhat against thee, because thou hast left thy first love. Remember therefore from whence thou art fallen, and repent, and do the first works; or else I will come unto thee quickly, and will remove thy candlestick out of his place, except thou repent.
>
> *—Revelation 2:2–5*

Kathe S. Rumsey

As a soldier of Christ, I must not get caught up in titles and church hierarchy. I must discern whether I can trust the words of the messenger. The messengers sent by God will never speak instruction that contradicts the Word of God. My Commander-in-Chief, Jesus Christ, has a battle plan that leads to victory every time. He sends His messengers to those on the frontlines of battle through the Holy Spirit. I must train my spiritual ears to hear Him.

God's Army Bible Boot Camp – Day 50

As I approach my final days of God's Army Bible Boot Camp, I pray I am more prepared and victorious over the enemy's skirmishes than when I began fifty days ago. All the answers I will ever need are found in my training manual, the Bible. I am now well-suited in God's whole armor. My Commander-in-Chief, Jesus Christ, continues to provide strategic marching orders through His Holy Spirit. I have ears to hear Him.

> He that descended is the same also that ascended up far above all heavens, that he might fill all things. And he gave some, apostles; and some, prophets; and some, evangelists; and some, pastors and teachers; for the perfecting of the saints, for the work of ministry, for the edifying of the body of Christ; till we all come in the unity of the faith, and of the knowledge of the Son of God, unto a perfect man, unto the measure of the stature of the fullness of Christ: that we henceforth be no more children, tossed to and fro, and carried about with every wind of doctrine, by the sleight of men, and cunning craftiness, whereby they lie in wait to deceive; but speaking the truth in love, may grow up into him in all things, which is the head, even Christ: from whom the whole body fitly joined together and compacted by that which every joint supplieth, according to the effectual working in the measure of every part, maketh increase of the body unto the edifying of itself in love.
>
> *—Ephesians 4:10–16*

Jesus is the One who assigns me to a specific position within God's army. I enlisted not realizing exactly what God would ask of me. Enlistment in the army of God is not for the double minded.

Not one of us knows how we will react to an attack of the enemy until we are tested. Daily, I renew my mind with the Word of God. I pray and find a way to move forward regardless of my circumstances. I must remind myself that overcoming adversity prepares me for the next encounter. I must never lose sight of God's mission. Jesus said, "These things I have spoken unto you, that in me ye might have peace. In the world ye shall have tribulation: but be of good cheer [courage]; I have overcome the world" *(John 16:33)*.

God's Army Bible Boot Camp – Day 51

> To the intent that now unto the principalities and powers in heavenly places might be known by the church the manifold wisdom of God, according to the eternal purpose which he purposed in Christ Jesus our Lord: in whom we have boldness and access with confidence by the faith of him.
>
> *—Ephesians 3:10–12*

God—through the death and resurrection of His Son Jesus Christ—redeemed His church. It is up to Jesus' church to declare and demonstrate to the principalities and powers in the heavenly places that Jesus possesses all authority both in heaven and on earth. In turn, Jesus has invested His power and authority to His church. *Ephesians 6:12* teaches me that my battles are not against flesh and blood. My battles are against the principalities, powers, rulers of the darkness of this world, spiritual wickedness in high places. I must put on the whole armor of God each day, so I can stand and conquer in the evil day.

God's Army Bible Boot Camp – Day 52

Am I prepared to serve God? I must test myself:

> And David inquired at the LORD; saying, Shall
> I pursue after this troop? Shall I overtake them?
> And he answered him, Pursue: for thou shalt surely
> overtake them, and without fail recover all.
>
> —*1 Samuel 30:8*

How many times does something happen and I react based upon my own wisdom and strength? As a soldier in the army of God I follow David's example and seek God for my military orders. Although conflicts manifest themselves here on earth, my battles are not with other people. *Ephesians 6:12* is a reminder to me, "For we wrestle not against flesh and blood, but against principalities, against powers, against the rulers of the darkness of this world, against spiritual wickedness in high places." If I desire to be victorious, I must seek God's wisdom. The Holy Spirit of God is currently speaking to the church. I now have ears to hear *(Revelation 2:29)*.

Prayers are being answered on a daily basis. God draws unbelievers into the midst of His people; some are hearing about Jesus Christ for the first time. The spiritually famished are all around me in this world. The enemy will do everything he can to stop me from being a godly witness. I must put on the whole armor of God daily and follow the teaching and training opportunities provided by the Holy Spirit.

As a soldier in God's army I must conduct my life differently than unbelievers. His armor is not of this world. He has provided me with the power and authority in the name of Jesus Christ to obtain victory here on earth. If I obey what the Holy Spirit is saying to me, I will be spiritually prepared for battle. Satan is looking for whom He may devour. Obedience of faith will prepare me spiritually, mentally, and emotionally for the battles in the heavenlies I face. God ordained the times and boundaries of my habitation *(Acts 17:26).* He would not have given me this assignment if He did not know that I could be victorious.

God's Army Bible Boot Camp – Day 53

Am I—as a believer, spiritually, mentally, and physically prepared—fitted with God's full armor so He can send me on assignment?

> Verily, verily, I say unto you, He that believeth on me [Jesus], the works that I do shall he do also; and greater works than these shall he do; because I go unto my Father.
>
> *—John 14:12*

This is a powerful verse. What works do I see Jesus doing in the Scriptures? The blind see, the lame walk, the sick recover, and much more.

Am I willing to obey God's Word? Have I matured in faith through hearing and obeying the rhema words of the Holy Spirit? Do I do the works that Jesus did? If not, why not?

In boot camp, soldiers experience realistic practice drills until they can boldly and confidently face their enemies. Likewise, God will train me through spiritual practice drills before He sends me into combat.

As a soldier in the army of God, I conduct my life differently than those of the world. I operate in a state of readiness at all times. If my Commander-in-Chief, Jesus Christ, calls me back into duty, I am ready to respond immediately with prayer.

God's Army Bible Boot Camp – Day 54

Am I spiritually, mentally, and emotionally prepared; fitted with the whole armor of God, so that God can use me according to His plan and purpose?

> Likewise the Spirit also helpeth our infirmities: for we know not what we should pray for as we ought: but the Spirit itself maketh intercession for us with groanings which cannot be uttered. And he that searcheth the hearts knoweth what is the mind of the Spirit, because he maketh intercession for the saints according to the will of God. And we know that all things work together for good to them that love God, to them who are the called according to his purpose.
>
> —*Romans 8:26–28*

No matter what is coming against me, God makes all these things work together for my good because I love Him and have been called according to His purpose. The hour has come for all believers to recognize the enemy for who he is *(Ephesians 6:12)*. Contrary to popular opinion, my enemies are not other people. No amount of security devises or diligent observation by neighbors can provide complete 24-hour protection. The army of God must submit to the leading of the Holy Spirit.

Three years ago, the serenity and peace of a neighborhood was shattered when a group of thieves broke into four homes while the owners were away at church, or on vacation. In each of these situations, other neighbors were watching the homes for their neighbors. This left many in the neighborhood with the realization that thieves come when you least expect them.

I have authority in the name of Jesus Christ to take back the territory the enemy attempts to control. I am part of God's occupying force here on earth. I must not forsake gathering with other believers. God provided His whole armor and His Holy Spirit for me. Jesus will not forsake me even to the end of the age. I must prepare for spiritual battles that are literally at my doorsteps. This is not the hour to give up, to run away, nor to hide. It is the hour to unite with other believers, to stand firm and face God's enemies. In military boot camp, soldiers experienced realistic practice drills until they can boldly face the enemy in confidence. God assigns practice drills to prepare me before He sends me on assignment.

God's Army Bible Boot Camp – Day 55

Am I prepared to serve God? I must test myself

I have been fitted with the whole armor of God, so I can be an effective prayer warrior for God's kingdom. "They shall call his name Emmanuel, which being interpreted is, God with us" *(Matthew 1:23)*. In the midst of my battles, God is with me. Jesus promised not to forsake me nor leave me even to the end of the age. As a good soldier, I must diligently follow the commands of my Commander-in-Chief, Jesus Christ.

As a soldier in the army of God, I must submit to the headship of Christ through the Holy Spirit. I have authority in the name of Jesus to take back the territory the enemy attempts to control. I am part of God's occupying force here on earth. I must not forsake assembling with other believers. God provided His whole armor and His Holy Spirit. Jesus will not forsake me. I must prepare for the spiritual battles that face me. Now is not the hour to grow weary and give up, nor hide. It is the hour to unite with other believers in the body of Christ. United, we stand strong and defeat God's enemies.

Kathe S. Rumsey

God's Army Bible Boot Camp – Day 56

Having learned to put on the whole armor of God, I am spiritually, mentally, and emotionally prepared with the basics of warfare. God provides me with everything I will ever need to be victorious.

Many in the church attempt to overcome the enemy in their own strength without understanding the armor God has already provided. My desire is to help others utilize the provisions our Commander-in-Chief—Jesus Christ—has already supplied.

My heart's prayer is that God's people will submit to Him and allow Him to use us where He has placed us. We—the church— are God's prayer warriors. As a member of His army, I must submit to the directives of the Holy Spirit. In the name of Jesus Christ, I have authority to overcome the world. I am part of the occupying force here on earth until Jesus returns.

God's Army Bible Boot Camp – Day 57

Not only have I learned to focus in prayer when the enemy attacks, but my friend has as well. Several years ago, her precious mother passed away. In addition to dealing with grief, she returned from a vacation to discover there had been a burglary, and her home was in shambles. She became terrified and anxious. The thieves broke into her home in broad daylight on a Sunday morning. Many in the neighborhood were attending church services or running errands. The very thought of this event became unsettling for everyone.

Shortly after my friend and I prayed together, God's peace was evident; she became more courageous. She continues to find things missing in her home but now is able through prayer to let everything go emotionally. Prayer changed her perspective. I could hear the difference in her voice. My friend told me she is no longer defeated by fear. She has learned to identify the spirit of fear. "For God hath not given us the spirit of fear; but of power, and of love, and of a sound mind" *(2 Timothy 1:7)*. She is a victorious overcomer!

My friend later told me she returned to her Bible each time the spirit of fear would try to overwhelm her. I could tell from the sound of her voice over the phone that she now understood what was necessary to be victorious. God is faithful *(2 Chronicles 20:15)*. I do not need to live in defeat, and neither do the people around me. To God be the glory!

Kathe S. Rumsey

Bible Boot Camp Has Ended

Time passed quickly! I have come to know other prayer warriors—soldiers of Christ—who have been trained and are ready to stand with me in prayer agreement against God's enemies.

In boot camp, soldiers experience valuable practice drills until they can boldly face their enemies with confidence. I have experienced practice drills in my life; they are not to destroy me—quite the contrary—they are to make me stronger in faith.

Through *God's Army Bible Boot Camp*, I pray others have learned to identify the spirit of fear and overcome the world *(2 Timothy 1:7; 1 John 5:4–5)*. In the midst of an enemy's attack, we can submit to God, resist the devil and he will flee *(James 4:7)*. As part of God's occupying force here on earth, Jesus' victory enables me to be more than a conqueror.

As a soldier—who has completed *God's Army Bible Boot Camp*—I have learned to conduct my life differently. God's armor and the weapons of my warfare are not of this world. In the name of Jesus Christ, I possess His power and authority to win every trial I face. Satan looks for whom he may devour. My battles are not against flesh and blood *(Ephesians 6:12)*. I choose to win—and with the Holy Spirit's help—I will overcome all the challenges the enemy plots against me *(Luke 22:15–18; Romans 14:16–19; Galatians 5:19–25)*.

Finally, My Brethren

Finally, my brethren, be strong in the Lord, and in the power of his might, Put on the whole armour of God, that ye may be able to stand against the wiles of the devil. For we wrestle not against flesh and blood, but against powers, against the rulers of the darkness of this world, against spiritual wickedness in high places. Wherefore take unto you the whole armour of God, that ye may be able to withstand in the evil day, and having done all, to stand. Stand therefore, having your loins girt about with truth, and having on the breastplate of righteousness; and your feet shod with the preparation of the gospel of peace; above all, taking the shield of faith, wherewith ye shall be able to quench all the fiery darts of the wicked. And take the helmet of salvation, and the sword of the Spirit, which is the word [rhema] of God; praying always and with all prayer and supplication in the Spirit, and watching thereunto with all perseverance and supplication for all saints, and for me, that utterance may be given unto me, that I may open my mouth boldly, to make known the mystery of the gospel.

—Ephesians 6:10–18

Kathe S. Rumsey

Personal Testimony

In October of 1983, I attended a Christian conference sponsored by a church in a nearby community. During this event, my life radically changed.

Prior to this conference, I considered myself a believer in God, and I knew of His Son Jesus Christ and the Holy Spirit of God, but I knew nothing about the Bible. I had *inherited* my faith—or so I realize now—from both sides of my parents' Christian families. I remember what a blessing it was to hear stories of my paternal praying grandmother. I never had an opportunity to meet her; she went home to heaven before I was born. When I spent the night at my maternal grandmother's, I recall as a child hearing her pray as I went to sleep next to her. When I awoke the next morning, I could still hear her praying.

If anyone would have asked me if I were going to heaven when I died, I would not have hesitated and replied, "Absolutely!" After all, when I prayed as a child, God answered my prayers. I knew He existed. What I did not know at the time was that His Son Jesus Christ had been viciously sacrificed at Calvary for all my sins. I also was unaware of the gift of the Holy Spirit—the Comforter—whom the Father sent to us at the request of Jesus.

As I walked into a gymnasium where a church congregation was to hold their conference, my worldly nature went into overdrive. I began to judge everything around me. The dissimilarity between this gym and the gloriously ornate churches I had attended was striking. Initially, I could not imagine that God would be present. Moments later, without musical accompaniment, the most beautiful sound began to flow from the center of the room. I had never heard anything so glorious in my life. I turned to ask my friend what was happening, and she said, "They are praying in their prayer languages." I did not know exactly what that meant at the time. However, I had to admit the same presence of God I had known as a small child had entered that room. After we sat down and the conference began, I looked around and realized everyone had their Bibles, pens, and notebooks in hand. I had not even thought to bring a piece of paper to write notes. When I turned to my friend, she had opened her Bible, and was reading. Self-conscious, I attempted to listen to the speaker, hoping no one would notice I did not have a Bible. A gentleman on my right asked what chapter and verse the speaker had referenced, so I turned to my friend to see if she knew. I did not even think to listen for Bible references.

When the speaker finished, he had an altar call for those who wished to receive a healing. I had not planned to go forward; we sat near the back row of chairs so I thought no one would notice us. Then I realized that every person on every row were proceeding forward. I panicked. I tried to think of something that needed to be healed and by now our row was next. As I slowly made my way, I was still trying to think of something. Then I remembered a few years earlier I had sprained my ankle, and occasionally, it gave me trouble. Whew!

The usher asked our row to line up in front of the pastor and his team of prayer ministers. The pastor began to pray for those on my right-hand side. There were about seven people before me. Out of my right peripheral view I noticed people falling backwards. One of the ladies in my Bible study once had mentioned being slain in the Spirit, so I decided I best keep my wits about me. Nervously, I started to wonder if I should excuse myself, get out of line, and leave the building. I was witnessing something I had never experienced previously. Then—almost before that thought cleared my mind—the pastor asked me if I would like prayer. I remember muttering something about an ankle sprain. He laid hands on my head and began praying in his prayer language. Immediately, I felt something—like a horizontal motion—going down layer upon layer inside my entire body from the top of my head to the bottom of my feet. When I walked back to my seat, I knew something had changed inside me spiritually, but I had no idea what it was.

The pastor's wife was the next speaker. I cannot tell you what she spoke about because I was still trying to understand what had just happened to me. I sensed God's presence in a room that should only have been used for sporting events. When the speaker finished, she had an altar call. She invited anyone who wished to receive the baptism with the Holy Spirit and their prayer language to raise their hand. By now, I was getting very nervous because my friend and I needed to get back home in time to meet our little girls' school bus. I turned to my friend to remind her we might want to leave now so we could return home in time. When I turned, I noticed her hand was the only one raised. The speaker asked everyone to continue to pray and wait. The Holy Spirit had given her a word that there was someone else. Fearing we would be separated, and I would lose my only ride back to our town, I slipped my hand up so we could stay together. The speaker immediately ended the prayer time. My friend and I were met by two ladies from the host church who escorted us to a room and prayed with us.

God knows me perfectly, and He knows my heart. Looking back, I realize this might have been my only opportunity to surrender to God's will and purpose for my life.

One of the church ladies explained the baptism with the Holy Spirit with the gift of a prayer language *(John 1:32–33)*. As she prayed for me, my prayer language began to flow *(John 7:37–39)*.

She gave me her card and offered to keep me in her prayers. I walked from the side-room to the gym and sat down in the back row. People mingled around the room speaking softly with one another. I felt God's precious presence enveloping me. I realized how filthy my sin of pride had been. God was not condemning my ignorance; His grace was sufficient.

Over the days that followed, I could not spend enough time in the Word of God. I wanted to pray in my new prayer language all day and night. For the first time in my life, I truly had peace. I began to realize that with God all things are possible. Previously, I always thought that with me, all things were possible. How foolish I had been.

Some members of my extended family immediately showed concern as they witnessed such a dramatic change in my conversation and behavior. I am sure they thought I had been brainwashed by a different denomination. It surprised me that my family did not seem comfortable with the changes in me. I was no longer selfish or manipulative. My heart's desire was to share the truth of God's Word like there was no tomorrow.

Thirty-seven years have passed since that significant event. My life has become an adventure that only Christ could have orchestrated. My priorities have changed. God has been faithful to me and to His Word that guides my life. I can never repay Him for the sacrifice He made on my behalf. I will use whatever talents He gives me to help the body of Christ mature and fulfill the role God has purposed for each one of us.

By His own blood, Jesus Christ purchased and redeemed His church. In Him, I am a victorious overcomer *(Revelation 12:10–11)*. As soldiers in the army of God, we have a choice to make. The church Jesus is building in America need not be—*The Powerless Church*—nor *America's National Disgrace*. The choice resides within the heart of each and every one of us!

About the Author

In the Fall of 1983, Kathe Rumsey's life was radically turned right-side-up following a series of relatively insignificant events: a class reunion, a neighborhood craft group that evolved into a Bible study. Through her determination to discover genuine purpose in life, she came to know Jesus Christ as her Lord and Savior. Kathe grew up in a Christian home and traditional denomination. Later, receiving the gift of the baptism with the Holy Spirit, she has undeniably experienced God's faithfulness. The Word of God is her Rock-solid basis for all her life choices. Kathe resides with her husband and family in Washington State.

Kathe S. Rumsey also coauthored with Roberta M. Wong:

- *Love Is the Commitment: Protocol Guidelines for God's Royal Wedding*

- *The Lamb's Wife Makes Herself Ready: Love Is the Commitment Bible Study and Workbook with Commentary*

- *Right-Side-Up in an Upside-Down World*

email contact: **tothe7churches@gmail.com**

Printed in the United States
By Bookmasters